THE PRACTITIONER IN~~QUIRY SERIES~~

Marilyn Cochran-Smith and Susan L. Lytle, SERIES EDITORS

Democratic Education in Practice:
Inside the Mission Hill School
MATTHEW KNOESTER

Action Research in Special Education: An Inquiry
Approach for Effective Teaching and Learning
SUSAN M. BRUCE & GERALD J. PINE

Inviting Families into the Classroom:
Learning from a Life in Teaching
LYNNE YERMANOCK STRIEB

Jenny's Story: Taking the Long View of the Child
—Prospect's Philosophy in Action
PATRICIA F. CARINI & MARGARET HIMLEY, WITH
CAROL CHRISTINE, CECILIA ESPINOSA, & JULIA FOURNIER

Acting Out! Combating Homophobia
Through Teacher Activism
MOLLIE V. BLACKBURN, CAROLINE T. CLARK,
LAUREN M. KENNEY, & JILL M. SMITH, EDS.

Puzzling Moments, Teachable Moments: Practicing
Teacher Research in Urban Classrooms
CYNTHIA BALLENGER

Inquiry as Stance:
Practitioner Research for the Next Generation
MARILYN COCHRAN-SMITH & SUSAN L. LYTLE

Building Racial and Cultural Competence in the
Classroom: Strategies from Urban Educators
KAREN MANHEIM TEEL & JENNIFER OBIDAH, EDS.

Re-Reading Families: The Literate Lives of Urban
Children, Four Years Later
CATHERINE COMPTON-LILLY

"What About Rose?" Using Teacher Research to
Reverse School Failure
SMOKEY WILSON

Immigrant Students and Literacy:
Reading, Writing, and Remembering
GERALD CAMPANO

Going Public with Our Teaching:
An Anthology of Practice
THOMAS HATCH, DILRUBA AHMED, ANN LIEBERMAN,
DEBORAH FAIGENBAUM, MELISSA EILER WHITE,
& DÉSIRÉE H. POINTER MACE, EDS.

Teaching as Inquiry: Asking Hard Questions to
Improve Practice and Student Achievement
ALEXANDRA WEINBAUM, DAVID ALLEN, TINA BLYTHE, KATHERINE
SIMON, STEVE SEIDEL, & CATHERINE RUBIN

"Is This English?" Race, Language, and
Culture in the Classroom
BOB FECHO

Teacher Research for Better Schools
MARIAN M. MOHR, COURTNEY ROGERS, BETSY SANFORD,
MARY ANN NOCERINO, MARION S. MACLEAN, & SHEILA
CLAWSON

Imagination and Literacy:
A Teacher's Search for the Heart of Learning
KAREN GALLAS

Regarding Children's Words:
Teacher Research on Language and Literacy
BROOKLINE TEACHER RESEARCHER SEMINAR

Rural Voices: Place-Conscious Education and the
Teaching of Writing
ROBERT E. BROOKE, EDITOR

Teaching Through the Storm: A Journal of Hope
KAREN HALE HANKINS

Reading Families:
The Literate Lives of Urban Children
CATHERINE COMPTON-LILLY

Narrative Inquiry in Practice:
Advancing the Knowledge of Teaching
NONA LYONS & VICKI KUBLER LABOSKEY, EDS.

Writing to Make a Difference:
Classroom Projects for Community Change
CHRIS BENSON & SCOTT CHRISTIAN, WITH
DIXIE GOSWAMI & WALTER H. GOOCH, EDS.

Starting Strong: A Different Look at
Children, Schools, and Standards
PATRICIA F. CARINI

Because of the Kids: Facing Racial and
Cultural Differences in Schools
JENNIFER E. OBIDAH & KAREN MANHEIM TEEL

Ethical Issues in Practitioner Research
JANE ZENI, ED.

(continued)

DEMOCRATIC EDUCATION IN PRACTICE

Inside the Mission Hill School

MATTHEW KNOESTER

FOREWORD BY
DEBORAH W. MEIER

Teachers College, Columbia University
New York and London

Published by Teachers College Press, 1234 Amsterdam Avenue, New York, NY 10027

Cover photos by Dani Coleman, Kathy D'Andrea, and Jenerra Williams

Library of Congress Cataloging-in-Publication Data

Knoester, Matthew, author.
  Democratic education in practice : inside the Mission Hill School / Matthew
    Knoester; foreword by Deborah Meier.
      pages cm. — (The practitioner inquiry series)
  ISBN 978-0-8077-5380-4 (pbk. : alk. paper) —
  ISBN 978-0-8077-5381-1 (hardcover : alk. paper)
    1. Mission Hill School (Boston, Mass.) 2. Democracy and education—
  United States. I. Title.
  LD7501.B6M445 2012
  372.9744'61—dc23   2012034873

ISBN 978-0-8077-5380-4 (paperback)
ISBN 978-0-8077-5381-1 (hardcover)

Printed on acid-free paper
Manufactured in the United States of America

19   18   17   16   15   14   13   12   8   7   6   5   4   3   2   1

Dedicated to the memory of five pillars of my family:

Eleanor A. R. Koster (1910–1999)
Clarence Koster (1911–1999)
Arie C. Knoester (1916–2002)
Akke Knoester (1922–2007)
Claybourn V. Brown II (1953–2012)

Contents

Foreword

I was driving from New York City to Boston to give a speech, I think, and my car radio wouldn't work. Three hours to think. I had already retired from the NYC public schools after 30 years in the system and was now an urban fellow at the Annenberg Institute in Providence, alongside Ted Sizer, Bruce Fuller, and Dennis Littky. As part of our fellowship we were paid to write and speak, separately and together, about school reform. It was an interesting combo, and when we traveled here and there to give talks about education, it was generally interesting.

But . . .

I missed being in a school, in a setting that involved so many possibilities and endless hopefulness. Each child, each family, and each colleague (not to mention the world that impacted on us) provided endless fascination and endless opportunities for observing colleagues and kids in action. This led in turn to constantly rethinking, chewing over new ideas, and gathering together to argue through new strategies—and of course there were the plain ordinary affections that had made those 30 years go by so fast. All those moments standing in the hall and listening to the buzz of school, the giggly children, the work all over the walls, the music coming from the end of the corridor, the friendly high fives between adults and students. Oh yes, there were those "other" moments: The angry parent, who had a good point, but . . . ; the ornery colleague who didn't agree with me; the sad child we couldn't reach; and the humiliation of having to outwit "downtown"—along with the triumphant times when we did.

By the time I got to Boston, I had decided. I was 65, and I had one more shot at doing what I loved best. Why not? It was time to go back to kindergarten and start over. Did children still dig to China? Did they still pretend to be kings and queens, explorers, and inventers of their own fairy tales?

I had a breakfast date with friends and education professors in Cambridge, Brenda Engel and Eleanor Duckworth. I parked my car and bounded in asking, "What do you two think about the idea of my starting a new public school here in Boston?" Instant excitement. We called Harvard professor and friend, Vito Perrone, who also loved the idea. I had known Tom Payzant, the Boston schools superintendent, for many years, so the next step would be talking with him. On our way to doing that we ran into Bob Pearlman, who was working for the local teacher's union. He told us that they had an agreement with the Boston school committee and Payzant to create Pilot schools—schools freed from most of the union/management contract. "Why not apply for that?" said Bob. Allen Graubard came on board to write the proposal, and all the pieces came together.

The next 9 years went by too fast. I had promised I'd stay until I couldn't walk up the stairs anymore. Well, I re-retired before that, but it turned out that walking down the steps was getting precarious. There were younger staff members ready to take over, and we needed to demonstrate that these kinds of schools didn't depend upon one person. I felt that many others could do the job—some even better.

I was right—even if there are times when it was hard to feel powerless and past experience (my own and others) hadn't always worked out well. The secondary school we started in New York City didn't survive the leadership transition by too many years. Still, Central Park East I and II in East Harlem have survived and thrived.

Today, nearly 15 years later, Mission Hill School remains on the way to being—there is never an end to this—the school I dreamed of. It's always been precarious. Who knows whether we'll survive the next educational fad or plan from the top—or if the policymakers, the billionaires, and the system will let us. The signs are not all good, as Matthew notes. The current absurd demand for Mission Hill School to move to a very different location and a realistically different physical plant doesn't seem like a good sign—but then signs are not always easy to read. I tend to be a paranoid optimist, and in this case I remain cautiously optimistic—though that is harder to be now that I am retired and watching from a distance.

What I miss now about teaching and the day-to-day life of the school is that if one does what's "right" (not always easy to figure out), one has an impact that can never be taken away. Every good day is one more good day in the life of a community of children and adults. Each day counts. And if it's a bad day, well tomorrow maybe one can undo harm done.

We are living through a difficult historic period. Many of the reforms I've been associated with all my life (and my family's) are being undermined. Leaders of our economy dare even talk about the drawbacks of democracy; "Maybe we need something like Singapore," I've heard said aloud by powerful people. The idea that ordinary people have a right to organize—into unions or even into street demonstrations!—seems shaky. Having fought war after war in the name of democracy, having fought against the idea that progress requires an authoritarian society—and won on both scores—we seem to have exhausted our enthusiasm for our victories. In the vacuum, greed and wealth and money have replaced the vision; all we need is a "free" marketplace where some win and some lose. The "winners" have declared that voting with dollars is equivalent to real actual human beings. Corporations are people?!

Matthew Knoester has done us an enormous favor by showing us, in detail, what *could be*—one example of how schools can be the building blocks for democracy, recreating community for all to taste, feel, hear, and see—with all the warts of any democratic community, but ready to learn to do it better. Where arguments are cherished, where being ignorant is always welcomed, a place where we can, despite the storms blowing outside, be safe enough to speak up or be silent—a place to know that what we do matters. We need these stories and we need to take them seriously. It's not a question of whether we need more Central Park Easts or Mission Hills—they are "only" examples of what can happen if we put our heads together, draw upon our highest aspirations, and create a community for ourselves, our children, and our colleagues. If we keep in mind that our schools are not for "other people's children," while also keeping in mind that "other people" may not always want for their child what we want for ours. Does that make it impossible? If so, then the whole idea of America is impossible.

I'm not ready to give up on that idea, even as I know the conundrum of democracy will never be solved. The entangled threads that hold us together will fray, over and over. And we will have to pick our way through all the knots, snarls, and broken ends to reinvent, revise, and respectfully agree to work together again to create a better world.

—Deborah W. Meier

Acknowledgments

There are many people I would like to thank here because they have supported this work in big and small ways before and during the process of writing this book. First, I would like to thank all of the current and former staff members of the Mission Hill School who have been wonderful colleagues and who volunteered to participate in this project, including Lukas Best, Jada Brown, Betsy Caruso, Maria Ceracola, Emily Chang, Dani Coleman, Kathy D'Andrea, Brenda Engel, Marla Gaines-Harris, Emily Gasoi, Ayla Gavins, JoAnne Hawkesworth, Beth Huston, Nakia Keizer, Alphonse Litz, Roberta Logan, Heidi Lyne, Laurel McConville, James McGovern, Geralyn Bywater McLaughlin, Deborah Meier, Amina Michel-Lord, Lakshmi Nayak, Letta Neely, Maura O'Toole, Jeanne Rachko, Ann Ruggeiro, Emily Schubin, Brian Straughter, Beth Taylor, Melissa Tonachel, Jenerra Williams, Jacob Wheeler, and John Wolfe. Thank you to Dani, Jenerra, and Kathy for the cover photographs. I would also like to thank all of the parents and graduates of the Mission Hill School who participated in this project. Since I promised anonymity I cannot list your names, but you know who you are! Thank you to the editors and reviewers at Teachers College Press, including John Bylander, Marilyn Cochran-Smith, Brian Ellerbeck, Nancy Power, Beverly Rivero, and Wendy Schwartz. Thank you especially to Susan Lytle for your enthusiasm about this project from the start.

Thank you to my Wisconsin community for your support in many ways, especially to Michael Apple, Wayne Au, Kristen Buras, Eduardo Cavieres, Minerva Chavez, Taina Collazo-Quiles, Ross Collin, Catherine Compton-Lilly, Christopher Crowley, Alexa Dimick, Joe Ferrare, Wangari Gichiru, Fatma Gok, Mary Louise Gomez, Carl Grant, Bryn Jaastad, Hee-Ryong Kang, Mi-Ok Kang, Ichiro Kuraishi, Gloria Ladson-Billings, Todd Lilly, Ching-Yu Lin, Assaf Meshulam, Linn Posey, Sarah Robert, Jorge Rodriquez, Jen Sandler, Mediha Sari, Katy Swalwell, Youl-Kwan Sung, Keita Takayama, Michael Thomas, Quentin Wheeler-Bell, Min Yu, and Wenfei Zhou. Thank you to the University of Evansville and especially to Lora Becker, Davies Bellamy, Robert Catena, Bob Ciscell, Dick Connolly, James Doane, Karen Doss, Sharon Gieselmann, Noah Gordon, Barbara Hahn, Vincent Harper, Walt Lewis, Amy McBride, Leanne Nayden, Jeannette

Oakley, Lynn Penland, Mari Plikuhn, Don Rodd, Bill Stroube, Lisa Toelle, Chuck Watson, and Terri Woolen for your support.

I would like to thank the great teachers I have had the pleasure of learning from in Grand Rapids, Northfield, Bogotá, and Cambridge, including Kathy Almgren, Anton Armstrong, David Booth, Nancy Fitzgerald, Mary Broene, Mauricio Barreto, Linda Burdell, Randy Buursma, Laurel Carrington, Noam Chomsky, Robert Coles, Eleanor Duckworth, Marty Grasmeyer, Terry Hoops, Susan Moore Johnson, Arie Knoester, Pedro Noguera, Randy Vellenga, Dirk Pegman, Gwen Pott, Mark Schelske, and Don Scott. Thank you to Laurie Gagnon and Roseann Tung at the Center for Collaborative Education in Boston for collaboration on planning and conducting interviews and making transcripts of interviews of particular graduates of the Mission Hill School. Thank you to the Coalition of Essential Schools for the Theodore R. Sizer Fellowship that supported this work.

Thank you to Dan Baker, Judith Bonifaci, Liz Canter, Carolyn Gramstorff, Derek Lee, Kirsten Peterson, Brad Simpson, Kristin Sundell, Beth Truesdale, Matt Wallen, and Christopher Wells for many conversations about the topics found in this book and about other topics prior to these. And thank you to my family: my parents, Julie and Bill Knoester, for your many years of support and your strong commitment to education; to my siblings,Chris, Ben, and Kathryn, for your love and support; to their spouses, Dana, Katie, Ben (And thank you Katie for the photo on the back cover!); to my sister-in-law, Amy Vance, for your community; to Mel and Linda Vance for your tremendous help in so many ways; to my late grandparents for so much, including sacrificing and risking a great deal to come to this country in the hope of providing a better life for your families; to my son and daughter, Nicolaus and Jubilee, for your love and much-needed distraction; and, above all, to my best friend and life partner, Carrie Vance, who is proud to have never read a single one of my articles or books before they were published—knowing the history of women's uncredited work—but who nevertheless has managed to provide lots of emotional and intellectual stimulation and support. Thank you!

DEMOCRATIC EDUCATION IN PRACTICE

*Inside the
Mission Hill School*

1

Introduction

But there's something else that's driving my commitment to public education—my passion for democracy and my fears for its future. Intolerance and dogmatism, narrow and often murderous national and religious loyalties, and the casual acceptance of the most grotesque inequities have made democracy's promise seem at times improbable rather than inevitable.

–Deborah Meier, *The Power of Their Ideas*, p. 5

This book is about a concrete and realistic alternative school model to the current dominant culture in education, which is characterized by a strong emphasis on standardized learning and testing within large impersonal schools. The current conditions have led to high dropout rates, unequal educational opportunities for students of color and from working-class families, and a narrowing of the curriculum to focus on technical skills for the workplace, rather than education for effective participation in a democracy and for personal and social transformation.

This book describes and evaluates a particular high-achieving school, the Mission Hill School, founded by Deborah Meier and colleagues in 1997, that has rethought almost everything about the schooling process. It is a small, racially and culturally integrated public pre-K–8 school using Dewey-influenced progressive education strategies and dedicated to educating students for democratic citizenship. Students are admitted to the school based on a lottery, and they graduate from the 8th grade after having produced and defended robust portfolios of student work in each subject. The waiting list for the school is long, graduates are generally admitted to the high schools of their choice, and 96.2% of the college-age graduates I surveyed for this book had entered college. It is a school worthy of close exploration by teachers, teacher educators, administrators, policymakers, and anyone interested in how to better understand seemingly intractable problems related to urban public education in the United States.

HOW I CAME TO THIS PROJECT

I was fortunate to be a long-term substitute teacher in a public elementary school in Roxbury, a neighborhood in Boston, and looking for a job, when I learned in 1997 that Deborah Meier was involved with opening a new school just blocks from where I was then teaching. In college, I had read Meier's (1995) first book *The Power of Their Ideas*, in which she recounted her experiences leading a small progressive school in East Harlem, New York. Her description of progressive education and her theories of student motivation resonated deeply with my experience. In fact, I had hoped and planned to visit her school in New York to learn more about it, so hearing that she would be starting a school in Boston was exciting news. As Meier recalled in her book, she helped to found several schools in New York, the most well known of which were the Central Park East Elementary School (K–6), started in 1974, and the Central Park East Secondary School (7–12), opened in 1985. Both schools were examined in depth by a variety of observers and scholars. In these studies, researchers described schools characterized by high levels of integration by race, culture, and class; the use of innovative and progressive curricula; shared decision making among staff; and wide community involvement in the schools (Bensman, 1987, 1994, 1995, 2000; Darling-Hammond & Ancess, 1993, 1994; Darling-Hammond, Ancess, & Faulk, 1995; Faust, 1993; Graff, 2003; Lappe, 2005; Lappe & Du Bois, 1994; Schmoker & Wilson, 1993; Seller, 1994; Shekerjian, 1990; Snyder, Lieberman, Macdonald, & Goodwin, 1992; Wood, 1992).

For example, David Bensman, a professor at Rutgers University, tracked down many of the graduates of Central Park East Elementary School, and found that CPE graduates were highly successful in high school and college, despite the high dropout rate of students in the New York City public schools (Bensman, 1994, 2000). Bensman also found that approximately 90% of Central Park East Secondary School graduates went on to college and stayed in college—an astounding number compared to the 50% dropout rate of New York high school students (Bensman, 1987, 1994, 1995). Meier received the prestigious MacArthur Fellowship for her work in New York City and turned her attention to the development of several advocacy groups before she decided once again to be intimately involved with opening a new school, this time in Boston.

I applied for a teaching job at the Mission Hill School the year it opened. I was fortunate to be offered a job in January of 1998 as an assistant teacher (a position some schools call paraprofessional) alongside a more experienced lead teacher, James McGovern. It was a wonderful, intense, and eye-opening experience, but I left the school after that 1st year, when no opening was available beyond my role as assistant. However, I returned to the school 3 years later, after teaching for 2 years at a nearby public elementary school and completing a Master of Education degree at Harvard University. This time I was hired as a lead teacher for a combined 4th- and 5th-grade classroom, where I stayed for 4 additional years.

Although I left the school in 2005 to pursue doctoral work, the Mission Hill School and the unique culture I witnessed and was a part of stayed with me. I began to write about the school, in articles, and eventually in doctoral work at the University of Wisconsin–Madison (Knoester, 2004, 2008, 2009, 2010, 2011a, 2011b, 2012). I described the theme-based curriculum I was involved in writing, which was focused on educating for democratic citizenship with substantial attention given to issues of social justice and anti-racism in a racially, culturally, and economically integrated setting. I wrote about the assessments we chose to use at Mission Hill, which were based on seeing the "whole child" by taking into consideration longitudinal data, along with innovative ways of evaluating students in various subjects and communicating with parents while avoiding the tracking and ranking of students that prevails in most schools. Upon reading my writing, members of my writer's group, for example, often responded with variations of the question, "Is what you describe *real?*"

What I understood from this question was not, "Does a school exist called 'the Mission Hill School'?" but rather, "Does the powerful learning community that you describe, interrupting the reproduction of inequalities—racial, economic, and otherwise—really work?" and "How do you know?"

THE NATURE OF THIS BOOK

Even as I taught at Mission Hill, and reflected on what I learned there, I wondered about these same questions. I know the staff, students, and others at Mission Hill worked hard. I know my colleagues and I spent many nights thinking and planning for our particular students. In these senses, the school was very "real." But to what ends were the time and work spent? How might the Mission Hill School evaluate itself, and might such an evaluation be useful or interesting to others?

Illuminating the Promise of the Mission Hill School

Although I include vignettes from my journal at the beginning of most chapters in this book from my time as a teacher in this school, the narrative found in these pages is not an autobiography, but an attempt by a former teacher at the school to discover and describe to what extent the promise of the Mission Hill School, a democratic and culturally integrated school, one that intentionally fights to interrupt the reproduction of racial, cultural, and economic inequalities, is "real." Since I am a former teacher in the school, I can offer a unique perspective, both with my own reflection and narrative, and also with the choices I make in asking 63 people who have also been intimately involved with the school, particular questions that may draw out answers with explanatory power, which illustrate the ways in which the Mission Hill School carries out its mission (Cochran-Smith & Lytle, 1993, 2009). Since I have taught in the school, as well as taught in and supervised student teachers in many other schools, I can see there are major differences between Mission Hill School and other schools. But I also know that telling the story of my own experiences in the school can only go so far in relating the "reality" of what makes the school unique.

For some readers, describing a school using the voices of graduates, parents, and staff may not be sufficiently persuasive evidence that the school successfully educates its students. I would be skeptical myself. For this reason, I also contacted graduates of the school to ask them to evaluate how their education at the Mission Hill School prepared them for high school. I found that students felt generally well prepared for high school, and of those who were college age at the time of the survey, 96.2% of the students who responded reported that they had entered college.[1] These findings appear to be roughly consistent with the findings of David Bensman, who conducted similar research of graduates of the Central Park East schools, also founded by Deborah Meier.

This book is also more than an introduction to the Mission Hill School. Due to the stature and respect earned by Deborah Meier in the field of education, Mission Hill School is already on the map of those familiar with educational literature. Meier herself has written about the school, in essays and articles, in a "blog debate" with Diane Ravitch, hosted by *Education Week* (Meier & Ravitch, 2012), and in six of her books (Meier, 1995, 2000, 2002; Meier, Engel, & Taylor, 2010; Meier, Sizer, & Sizer, 2004; Meier & Wood, 2004; for a complete listing of Meier's publications see Meier, 2012). Newspaper reporters have written about the school, and many educators have sought out and visited the school personally. Six current or former teachers have written reflections about their teaching and participation in the life of the school (McLaughlin, 2005, 2009, 2012; Gasoi, 2009, 2011; Gavins, 2005; Knoester, 2004, 2008; Lyne, 2005, 2010a, 2010b; Williams, 2011); one former principal wrote a doctoral dissertation on the topic of peer review at the Mission Hill School (Straughter, 2001), and another former teacher has just completed a doctoral dissertation comparing decision-making processes at the Mission Hill School with those of a KIPP charter school (Gasoi, 2012).

Despite all this literature, no reviews of the Mission Hill School to date present the voices of a large number of staff members, graduates, and parents; or marshal a robust theoretical framework that contextualizes the school and its practices in the empirical and theoretical literature on democratic education, urban education, critical educational studies, race, class, gender, curriculum studies, assessments, and professional development.

Exploring the Unique Traits of Mission Hill School

As a way of demonstrating why the Mission Hill School deserves an in-depth description, I point to three of the most immediately visible of the unique traits of the Mission Hill School, often discussed in the publications noted above, and each worth book-length explorations of their own:

1. The school is small—only about 170 students attend—How does this feature offer opportunities and limitations?[1]
2. The school is racially integrated—The current demographics of the school are 41.4% Black, 27.8% Hispanic, 22.8% White, 0.6% Asian, 7.4% mixed or other. Elementary school averages in the Boston Public Schools are 33.7% Black, 12.6% White, 43.0% Hispanic, 8.3% Asian, and 2.3% other (Boston Public Schools, 2012; Massachusetts Department of Elementary and Secondary Education, 2012). How is this achieved in a setting, like Boston, that is severely segregated?
3. The school is one of 21 *pilot schools* in the Boston Public Schools, which means that Mission Hill, much like many charter schools, enjoys autonomy in five key areas: governance, hiring, schedule, budget, and curriculum (Center for Collaborative Education, 2009; Knoester, 2011a). What opportunities and challenges present themselves with these autonomies?

It is tempting to choose just one of these aspects of the school for analysis, since each is quite rare and difficult to achieve in many political contexts. However, such a study would lose the proverbial forest for the trees, in focusing on too few of the aspects that make the whole school. In fact, many excellent studies have been carried out focusing on the positive educational impact of small school size (Ayers, Klonsky, & Lyon, 2000; Raywid, 1997, 1999, 2006), the importance and rarity of culturally integrated school settings (Kozol, 2005; Orfield & Eaton, 1996), and the advantages that pilot schools enjoy in the Boston Public Schools, and in other settings where such autonomies exist (Center for Collaborative Education, 2009; Knoester, 2011a).

As I list some of the basic elements that set Mission Hill School apart from so many other schools, it becomes clear that the school deserves more than a cursory introduction, or a study of just one aspect of the school. While each of the characteristics listed above deserves careful evaluation, and are features of the school that enable other important approaches to occur, not one of them is a panacea, nor can they fully describe the Mission Hill School.

The Mission Hill School is a complex institution, made up of unique individuals, a school culture, and structural and curricular strategies that operate as multiple moving parts, none of which are easy to evaluate individually, but together create a powerful combination. If Mission Hill School has anything to teach those who care about schools and education, which I believe it does, the school deserves an in-depth treatment, evaluating and describing the pragmatics and rationale of its approach. This study is designed to ask, "How does Mission Hill *use* its relative autonomies and other structural advantages?" Smallness, racial integration, and pilot status are important structural features, but they do not automatically make a school democratic, or able to interrupt the reproduction of inequalities in society based on race, class, or gender.

The investigation that informs this book's conclusions employs a variety of methods to evaluate and describe the school, including a rich tapestry of interviews with 63 staff, parents, and graduates of Mission Hill School, as well as surveys of additional graduates of the school.

THE CENTRAL ARGUMENT OF THE BOOK

In order to contextualize the school and better understand the significance of what I describe, I provide a theoretical argument rooted in a particular notion of democratic education. Democratic education is the centerpiece of the theory, in part because it is at the heart of the mission statement of the Mission Hill School. However, I also argue that theoretical work done by scholars in the area of democratic education, especially those who differentiate *thick* from *thin* democracy, marshaling a robust critique of marketization, provide some of the most important groundwork for understanding how inequalities in education can be understood and interrupted (Apple, 2006; Apple & Beane, 2007; Barber, 2003; Dewey, 1927). The title of this book includes the term *in practice* because it is unlike philosophical work in these areas, as this book is not pure theory or a description of an idealized setting. It is a description of a real, imperfect, and sometimes contradictory school. And my data and analysis here include less than perfect descriptions of the institution, as well as accounts of what I see to be difficult dilemmas within the school. My hope is that my description and analysis will point to both promising practices as well as provoke critical reflection on the dilemmas of choosing a particular set of educational approaches, focusing on the goal of education for effective democratic citizenship.

The main argument of the book is that since powerful forces of inequality and suppression exist within our society, leading to the reproduction of social inequalities in and by schools, a democratic school must be aware of, and continuously thoughtful, innovative, and courageous in counteracting these forces. The book demonstrates that Mission Hill School staff members recognize these challenges, which I outline in more depth in Chapter 2. They have designed the school to accomplish this task, so students are better able to learn the "habits of mind" that frame the curricular goals of the school.

REASONS WHY MISSION HILL SCHOOL IS WORTH EXAMINING

There are moreover nine key reasons the Mission Hill School is worth a careful examination:

1. The academic success of the graduates of the school is exemplary. This is unusual for an urban public school with a lottery-based admission system. However, the academic success is measured not primarily by test scores, which are above the city's averages, but are not exemplary. The more powerful evidence is the following: the rate of college-age graduates attending college is approximately 96% of those who responded to my survey, the rich descriptions of the portfolios students develop and defend before an evaluation committee before graduating, impressive academic feats achieved by students throughout their schooling process, the students' descriptions of their successful high school experiences, parents' descriptions of their children's successes, and the descriptions from each of the constituents interviewed of the power of the portfolio process and other academic work of students attending the school.

2. The Mission Hill School is a rare example of a racially and culturally integrated school. The work of Gary Orfield and others at the Civil Rights Project, for example, demonstrates that schools in the United State are as segregated today as they were 50 years ago, and schools in the Boston area are highly segregated (Orfield, 2009). It is important to ask and learn from this school: How do staff members and others involved think about, value, and strategize around these issues?

3. The founder of the school, Deborah Meier, has compiled a long track record of success that alone makes this school worth examining. Meier has helped to found five schools in Harlem, New York, and Boston that are some of the most-researched schools in the United States. (Bensman, 1987, 1994, 1995, 2000; Darling-Hammond & Ancess, 1993). The Mission Hill School is the last school Meier has helped to found, having learned many lessons from her previous endeavors, but

Mission Hill School has not been examined closely. Imagining a world that is not driven by high-stakes testing does not have to be imagining a utopia; we can learn from schools that currently exist and have prospered, despite the headwinds of test-based assessments that have made achieving their missions more difficult, rather than easier.

4. The Mission Hill School is a rare example of an urban school implementing Dewey-influenced progressive pedagogy. One of the central critiques of progressivism in education is that it can be found only in elite private schools, or that it is ineffective for poor children or children of color (Bernstein, 1977; Delpit, 1995). The Mission Hill School, along with other schools founded by Meier, is a powerful counter-example to these perceptions.

5. The Mission Hill School uses pedagogy and curricula that can be described as anti-racist and culturally relevant to its student body. This pedagogy and approach has a strong theoretical underpinning in current educational literature (Banks & McGee Banks, 2009; Gay, 2010; Grant & Gomez, 2001; Ladson-Billings, 1995, 2006; Perry, Steele, & Hilliard, 2003; Valdes, 1996; Valenzuela, 1999). However, it is too rarely found in schools, which are dominated by standards-based and test-driven curricula.

6. The Mission Hill School is a small school and uses its smallness in interesting ways, including shared decision making and intensive problem solving among a small group of teachers, parents, and students, and weekly meetings of the whole school to share student work.

7. The Mission Hill School is an internally democratic, largely teacher-governed school, a distinct view of what democratic education means, and worth a close examination. This form of decision making forms a model and assists with the mission of the school, which is to produce powerful democratic citizens, as opposed to focusing solely on education for future workers, although there are clearly overlaps between these goals.

8. The school is a pilot school within the Boston Public Schools, a unique collaboration between the teacher union and the school district, allowing more autonomy on the part of the school to think "outside of the box" when designing curriculum, making budgetary decisions, and addressing various challenges, an interesting model, but not without drawbacks (Knoester, 2011a).

9. As was mentioned previously, none of the books about schools associated with Meier were written by teachers in the schools under study. A teacher in the school has an insider perspective, and can ask questions of participants that are designed to draw out unique aspects

of the school and can flesh out particular topics that only someone spending large amounts of time in the school could do (Cochran-Smith & Lytle, 1993, 2009). A critical reader may charge that a teacher writing about his or her own school would be biased toward its success, and I have thought carefully about that perception throughout this process. But since I am writing about a school founded by a person whose work is well researched, the work described here can be compared and corroborated with the work conducted by outside researchers examining the Central Park East schools, and would be found to be consistent with that work, while also offering important and unique perspectives.

WHAT IS AND IS NOT COVERED HERE

It may also be helpful to caution the reader that various important topics are beyond the scope of this book. For example, this book does not include a full explication of social problems, their roots, and their causes. It is not a description of how to scale up the model of one particular school to remake an entire district or large group of schools. It is not a full analysis of school-choice models, such as pilot schools in Boston, or of unionization in education, although, as a pilot school, the Mission Hill School is part of a hybrid public-choice program with unionized teachers. As I describe in the book, pilot schools are given particular affordances, but they are not a panacea, a topic I have written much more about elsewhere (Knoester, 2011a). This book is not a full defense of public education and the public sector, and it does not provide a step-by-step guide on how to run a Dewey-influenced, progressive-education–style classroom. Nor does this book include a full analysis of what democracy means within education or even whether democracy is possible in an unequal society.

All of these topics are certainly worthy of close examination and study, and although readers of previous drafts of this work have expressed hope that these topics might be given a full treatment in this book, I would be remiss if I implied that these topics receive a fair exploration here. Instead, this book is a close examination of one small, personalized school and an analysis of why particular decisions are made at the school. The focus here is particularly on the unique aspects of the school, including

- the creation of a close school community across cultural divides;
- whole-school decision-making processes;
- whole-school, 3-month thematic units;

- the range of assessments used at the school, including portfolio presentations;
- professional development and capacity building within the school; and
- basic approaches to curriculum at various levels of child development.

This book focuses on school-level approaches to building a respectful and inclusive intellectual community, and the development of democratic "habits of mind," and descriptions of particular classroom activities are offered as examples in this regard. I insert citations throughout this book to point to books and other sources where more in-depth treatments of the various topics raised above can be found, which may assist readers who are looking for deeper analyses or more detailed descriptions of topics beyond the scope of this book.

I would also like to note that I have tried to write this book with at least two audiences in mind. First, this book is for school leaders, including teachers, who may be interested in the work of Deborah Meier and in urban progressive education more generally. I imagine that these readers are interested in the detailed descriptions of how the Mission Hill School is organized, how the school community has addressed particular problems found in urban public schools, and the results of surveys and interviews with graduates, parents and staff. I imagine this audience is less interested in the theoretical underpinnings of the school and of the theoretical arguments I make in these pages.

The second audience for this book is educational scholars and graduate students who are familiar with, or curious about, the citations to other educational research found here. I imagine they will be interested in the theoretical arguments found in this book, which build on work in critical and democratic educational theory, progressive educational theory, multicultural educational theory, assessment theory, and school leadership theory.

ORGANIZATION OF THE BOOK

This book is organized as follows: In Chapter 2 I introduce the theoretical argument and provide a definition of a democratic education and suggest why providing such an education is tremendously difficult. Readers who see themselves as part of the first audience described above may want to skip the second chapter and move directly to the third. Chapter 3 describes the founding of the school, the various political forces that converged to enable the school to open, and challenges that the founders faced as they opened a new school. Chapter 4 describes the challenge of creating a trusting integrated school community in a deeply segregated school system and the many actions taken by the school to address these challenges. Chapter 5 describes the processes of shared decision making used at the school among the various constituencies, focusing on the governing board and the faculty senate. Chapter 6 describes basic approaches to curriculum at each developmental level at the Mission Hill School, and provides rationales for these approaches. Although it is the longest chapter, it should not be taken as a step-by-step guide for how to teach in a Mission Hill School style, but rather will offer examples of classroom activities and theory drawn from teachers at the school, as well as both positive and critical reviews of the curriculum from parents and graduates. In Chapter 7 I focus on assessment at Mission Hill, including formative and summative assessments of student learning, the portfolio process that 7th- and 8th-graders complete before graduation, and how teachers communicate with parents about student assessments. Chapter 8 focuses on professional development and building a culture of teacher inquiry and critical reflection, drawing largely from interviews with teachers and with Deborah Meier.

In each of these chapters, I draw on interviews with teachers and staff, parents, and graduates of the school, as well as reflect on my personal experience at the school, to describe how decisions have been made and how the school has affected the lives of participants.

In the final chapter, I return to major themes and imagine what the future holds for the Mission Hill School. The school will be moving to a new location, for example, and adding more students due to its popularity, despite strong resistance from the school community to uproot. New challenges are on the horizon for the school, and, like most important topics, more research will be needed on the themes raised in this book.Reflections on these topics are included in chapter 9.

2

What Is Democratic Education and Why Is It So Difficult to Provide?

> I know no safe depository of the ultimate powers of the society but the people themselves; and if we think them not enlightened enough to exercise their control with a wholesome discretion, the remedy is not to take it from them, but to inform their discretion by education.
>
> –Thomas Jefferson

This chapter makes an argument for the purposes of public education in a democracy, lays out the major problems schools face in creating equal and effective educational opportunities for students, and points to promising directions for creating democratic schools. These arguments are crucial for understanding the work of the school under focus here.

The Mission Hill School, which I view as a model of inclusive and responsive democratic education, has explicitly stated in its mission statement that the purpose of the school is to help students become effective democratic citizens. But this is not a random goal. Helping students become effective citizens is arguably the most defensible reason for providing, investing in, and improving public schools, as articulated by founders and pioneers of public education in the United States, including Horace Mann, and others (Mann, 1989). However, democracy and democratic education are sliding signifiers (Foner, 1998), having different meanings for different people, so this book describes a specific model of democratic education, that of the Mission Hill School, and draws from theoretical work on democratic and critical democratic education to reach a deeper understanding of the rationale of the school.

In one interview with the founding principal of Mission Hill School, Deborah Meier, I asked how she defined a democratic school. She replied, "It is one where you're continuously exploring how everybody's voice can be heard, and acted upon, effectively." This book will evaluate and describe this "continuous exploration."

In this chapter I first present the mission statement of the school, which outlines the goals of an education for powerful democratic citizenship. I then present five major current challenges to the provision of this form of democratic education. Along with each I provide research literature pointing to promising alternative paths for addressing them. This literature—consisting of critiques of what currently exists and theoretical alternatives—will provide a conceptual base for contextualizing and understanding the description and evaluation of the Mission Hill School that I present in the following chapters.

THE MISSION OF THE SCHOOL

The founding faculty of the Mission Hill School thought carefully about how they would articulate their mission. They wrote an unusually long but vivid and powerful vision for the purpose of education in a democratic society. The mission statement is worth quoting in full:

> The task of public education is to help parents raise youngsters who will maintain and nurture the best habits of a democratic society: be smart, caring, strong, resilient, imaginative and thoughtful. It aims at producing youngsters who can live productive, socially useful and personally satisfying lives, while also respecting the rights of all others. The school, as we see it, will help strengthen our commitment to diversity, equity and mutual respect.
>
> Democracy requires citizens with the capacity to step into the shoes of others, even those we most dislike, to sift and weigh alternatives, to listen respectfully to other viewpoints with the possibility in mind that we each have something to learn from others. It requires us to be prepared to defend intelligently that which we believe to be true, and that which we believe best meets our individual needs and those of our family, community and broader public—to not be easily conned. It requires also the skills and competencies to be well informed and persuasive—to read well, to write and speak effectively and persuasively, and to handle numbers and calculations with competence and confidence.
>
> Democracy requires citizens who are themselves artists and inventors—knowledgeable about the accomplishments, performances, products and inventions of others but also capable of producing, performing, and inventing their own art. Without art we are all deprived.
>
> Such *habits of mind*, and such competence, are sustained by our enthusiasms, as well as our love for others and our respect for ourselves,

and our willingness to persevere, deal with frustration and develop reliable habits of work. Our mission is to create a community in which our children and their families can best maintain and nurture such democratic habits.

Toward these ends, our community must be prepared to spend time even when it might seem wasteful hearing each other out. We must deal with each other in ways that lead us to feel stronger and more loved, not weaker and less loveable. We must expect the most from everyone, hold all to the highest standards, but also respect our different ways of exhibiting excellence. We must together build a reasonable set of standards for our graduates so that they can demonstrate to us their capacity to meet this mission. (Mission Hill School, 2012)

This mission statement articulates an ambitious set of goals for any school. But how does a school go about achieving such a mission? What structures need to be in place? What are the knowledge, skills, and dispositions needed by the staff of the school? What are the dangers and pitfalls along the way? And what has the school learned from experience in attempting to achieve its mission?

These questions will be explored for the remainder of this book. However, before I describe the pragmatics of how the school responds to these questions I first present an argument on why this mission is important, what are the powerful forces opposing its achievement, and why particular pedagogical strategies are more likely to be consistent with the mission statement than others.

In order to educate democratic citizens it is important to create a school that is internally democratic—that practices what it hopes to teach. In the following section I draw on the work of Amy Gutmann, Benjamin Barber, and Michael Apple, among others, to articulate a theory of the basic elements of a democratic school, one that is mindful of the forces of inequality in a capitalist society to prevent students, particularly from oppressed and marginalized groups, from receiving a powerful education for democratic citizenship.

WHAT IS DEMOCRATIC EDUCATION?

Arguably the most influential current scholar who has considered issues of democratic education is Amy Gutmann (1999). Gutmann outlined three major views held by philosophers—most notably, Plato, Locke, and Mill, regarding the stakeholders best capable of making key decisions regarding the education of youth outside of the home. The three views she names are, respectively, the Family State, the State of Families, and the State of Individuals. Gutmann argues that in each of these views its proponents assume either the state, families, or individuals should take the leading, or even an exclusive, role in making decisions about schooling (Gutmann, 1999, pp. 19–32).

Gutmann then proposes a democratic model, which, in contrast to the three historical positions named above, consists of shared decision making among the key stakeholders in education, bound by two basic principles, that of nonrepression, which means a situation that prevents students and teachers from discussing competing notions of "the good life," and nondiscrimination, which means all students must be given the opportunity of an effective education.[1] These principles hold that particular stakeholders cannot overstep their bounds, that a central purpose of public education is teaching children rational deliberation among various views of the "good life" and this goal shall not be inhibited, that all children have the right to be educated, and that all stakeholders in public education must cede at least some control of educational decision making to professional educators (Gutmann, 1999, pp. 41–47).

Critical Democratic Education

Gutmann's theory broadly and effectively outlines and defends essential principles necessary for an inclusive school and school system. However, when a broad theory meets particular schools and communities, it is important to be prepared with more than ideals. What is also needed when discussing the particularities of how a school should operate is a more finely articulated critique of the challenges that currently exist to an inclusive and responsive democratic education—including some challenges that are deeply seated and even rooted in unconscious assumptions—that make the goals of democratic education difficult or impossible to achieve. Only then may effective strategies for how to address these problems become apparent.

For example, scholars in the critical educational theory tradition(s) have shown that racial, cultural, and economic segregation and tension; unequal funding; inadequate resources; ineffective teaching methods; and dysfunctional institutions and school leadership have plagued public school systems, including the Boston Public Schools, making democratic education as outlined by Gutmann out of reach (Anyon, 1997, 2005; Apple, 1988, 1995, 2006; Apple, Au, & Gandin, 2009; Darder, Baltodano, & Torres, 2008; Formisano, 2004; Freire, 1970, 1974, 1995, 2005; Giroux, 1988, 2001; hooks, 1994; Jan, 2007; Kozol, 1967, 2005; Lipman, 1998, 2004; McLaren, 2006; Noguera, 2003; Rothstein, 2004; Valenzuela, 1999).

These critical scholars, among others, have outlined central tensions and tendencies preventing schools and their graduates from benefiting from a level playing field, and have served to deprive particular students, especially those of poor or working-class families and African American students, among other marginalized and oppressed groups, of opportunities available to those of mainstream White middle-class or upper-class families. Specifically, researchers have pointed to the high rates of high school noncompletion, high rates of suspensions and expulsions, disproportionate levels of students of color in special education classrooms, rigid tracking in schools, low levels of college entrance, and inequalities in funding and resources such as experienced teachers (Anyon, 1997, 2005; Darling-Hammond, 2010; Fine, 1991; Lipman, 1998, 2004; Kozol, 1992, 2005; Rothstein, 2004). These problems clearly violate Gutmann's principles of nonrepression and nondiscrimination, which are essential for democratic education.

Schooling in a Capitalist Society

A full inquiry into the roots of these problems would have to include an in-depth analysis of capitalism and the persistent economic inequalities it produces, as well as the long history of racism, classism, and patriarchy that has characterized many aspects of U.S. society, all having powerful effects within schools (Apple, 1988, 1995, 2004, 2006; Bourdieu, 1984; Bourdieu & Passeron, 1977; Gilligan & Richards, 2008; Mills, 1999). However, to narrow the scope of this inquiry, and to provide a context for understanding the specific educational approaches of the Mission Hill School, I will focus here on five major challenges to democratic education in the United States. Compared with the more overarching problems inherent with capitalism, racism, and patriarchy, the problems I focus on here may seem like mere symptoms. Nevertheless, because these problems have become what Gramsci (1971) might have called hegemonic and what Apple (1995) called "common sense" aspects of U.S. schooling, the current structure of schooling, although problematic, is so common that it is seen as inevitable. In fact, there have been layers of political rationale explaining why the educational approaches that produce current outcomes are inevitable.

Defenders of these pedagogical approaches may argue that rigidly tracking students in ability groups, for example, addresses the problems of inequality and suppression listed above, such as the problem of high levels of high school noncompletion; or they may argue that there are simply no alternatives to this way of structuring schooling (Apple & Beane, 2007). Apple (2006) and others (Anyon, 1997, 2005; Lipman, 1998) have argued that, given the counter-pressures, counter-hegemonic work in education (including schooling that defies common practice and produces more-equal and effective outcomes) is extremely difficult to achieve and perhaps cannot be maintained without a social movement to support it. Schools are just one part of society so, following Anyon (2005), I do not care to be romantic about the power of schools alone to create a just society, as unequal power relations are ubiquitous in a capitalist society. Nevertheless, these five critiques of the current state of schooling in the United States are important since the concerns they address powerfully affect the lives of real students and families.

FIVE KEY CHALLENGES TO DEMOCRATIC EDUCATION

Here I outline five key challenges to democratic schooling, and provide theoretical work that points toward alternative approaches to schooling that are more likely to lead to education for democratic citizenship. The five key challenges to democratic schooling are as follows:

1. Schools are too often culturally insensitive and disrespectful to the diverse constituencies they serve.
2. Schools are too often indifferent and unresponsive to the specific desires of their constituencies, especially constituencies of working-class parents of color, when being more responsive (through the use of shared decision making, for example) could elicit a stronger sense of ownership and trust on the part of parents and community members.
3. Schools are too often heavily focused on the control of students, causing schools to resemble and function like prisons, especially those urban schools serving Black and economically disadvantaged students.
4. Schools too often rely on a reductionist and simplistic view of children, teachers, and schools, placing high value on flawed and misleading tests.
5. Schools too often place little value and offer too little support for the relationship between the teacher and student—the central relationship at the heart of teaching and learning—investing little trust in the professional knowledge of teachers and dedicating few resources toward the growth and development of the educational judgment of teachers.

Later in this book, these five problems will be juxtaposed, one by one, with the alternative educational approaches offered by the Mission Hill School. In Chapter 4, for example, I describe the Mission Hill School's response to the first challenge listed above. In Chapter 5, I describe the Mission Hill School alternative to the second challenge. In Chapter 6, I describie the Mission Hill alternative to the third challenge, and so on.

Schools as Culturally Insensitive

A growing number of critical scholars have pointed to the many ways in which schools are often insensitive and disrespectful to the diverse constituencies they serve (Anyon, 1997; Au, 2009; Banks & McGee Banks, 2009; Delpit, 1995; Gay, 2010; Grant & Gomez, 2001; hooks, 1994; Kozol, 1967, 2005; Ladson-Billings, 1995, 2006; Lawrence-Lightfoot, 2003; Lipman, 1998; Perry, Steele, & Hilliard, 2003; Valdes, 1996; Valenzuela, 1999). These insensitivities are not usually overt statements, but part of what Apple (2004) and others call the "hidden curriculum" of sending messages to students and parents alike that they are not welcome in the school and that school is not for people "like them." Examples include a school staff consisting entirely of White faces while the school population is ethnically diverse, the celebration of holidays in the school that represent the culture or religion of one group while marginalizing others, a curriculum that legitimates the knowledge and achievements of one group of people while delegitimizing the contributions of others, the scheduling of meetings and other events when many parents are at work, the refusal to greet parents as they enter the building, and the treatment of family members as unwanted intruders.

The theorists named above have argued that this insensitive manner of treating culturally diverse parents and students is far from inevitable. Alternatives include choosing to visibly value the cultures of all students in the school, including making explorations of culture, race, and inequalities a central part of the curriculum. Schools can and should consider how they are perceived through the eyes of parents and students from diverse cultures. What messages are sent to visitors from what is hanging on the walls? Is a friendly face greeting parents as they enter the office or school building? Are curricular gatherings scheduled at convenient times? Are communications sent home to parents in ways that are accessible? Are parents heard and respected when they approach school staff or attend meetings or events, or are their opinions sought even if they cannot attend meetings? Some schools provide or arrange for food during events at the school. And schools can provide a range of ways for parents and families to become involved with the life of the school. These questions and set of topics will be explored in much greater depth in Chapter 4, where I describe the ways in which the Mission Hill School has considered and addressed these crucial issues.

Schools as Instruments for Serving Consumer Preferences

One of the most powerful current challenges to implementing more democratic policy reforms is the ideology of *neoliberalism*. This ideology views schools, including public schools, as a commodity serving consumer preferences, wherein the consumers are the parents. Growing to dominance in the early 1980s, neoliberalism is characterized by the belief that an open market leads to prosperity for the greatest number of people; some even claim it is a democratic form of economy and governance, maximizing responsiveness to consumers (Apple, 2006; Apple & Beane, 2007; Barber, 2003; Calvert, 1993; Gomes & Unger, 1996; Harvey, 2005; Knoester, 2011a; Weiner, 2005). Neoliberalism has strongly affected debates about schooling in the United States, and a neoliberal agenda has been supported by legislators from both the Republican and Democratic parties (Bolick, 2006; Hoff, 2008).[2]

When viewed through the lens of democratic education, two key errors with arguments for market-based school reforms become apparent. The first is that they depend on a romantic notion of how a single powerful administrator can bring about democratic reforms, if only unencumbered with such "bureaucratic" concerns as collaborative deliberation and decision making, collective bargaining, and respect for job protections such as due process. Whereas in fact, many attacks on "bureaucracy," in neoliberal parlance, target essential elements crucial to ensuring a more inclusive and democratic set of institutions, such as investing the time necessary to follow agreed-upon work contracts and building a school culture that ensures nondiscriminatory work practices (Apple, 2003, 2004, 2006; Johnson & Landman, 2000).

The second key error is that in place of a strong democratic and deliberative model of schooling—one capable of providing inclusive and effective education for students and families—neoliberalism advances what Gutmann (1999) refers to as the "State of Families" view of education, in which proponents of market-based reforms insist parents are the primary authorities on decisions regarding public schools (Finn, Manno, & Vanourek, 2001; Lubienski, 2003; Schneider, Teske, & Marschall, 2000; Vergari, 2007).

In a neoliberal view of education, schools are placed in the position of service provider for consumers, who are the parents. As schools compete for market position, school choice proponents argue schools are pressured to be more responsive to parents.[3] However, the question of inclusion is undervalued, replaced with possessive individualism. In a market, only those with capital can purchase only those items available. But what may not be available is a rich, diverse, inclusive, functional democratic community focused on education for future democratic citizens, a community animated not by possessive individualism, but by thoughtful deliberation, grounded in principles of inclusion and responsiveness.[4] Apple (2006) argues,

> Our more political and collective understandings of democracy are currently under attack, often more than a little successfully. These new definitions of democracy are largely based on possessive individualism, on the citizen as only a "consumer," and are inherently grounded in a process of deracing, declassing, and degendering. (p. 114)

By contrast, a democratic model of education that directly addresses inequalities in schools is what Apple (2006) refers to as *thick* democracy, as opposed to the *thin* democracy of markets, individualism, and consumerism—the current common-sense thinking about how to best distribute education in a capitalist society. The thin democracy of markets may offer a particular form of responsiveness to parents, and this promise is a powerful reason some are attracted to the idea of school vouchers and for-profit charter schools. However, the question of inclusion is greatly undervalued.

Barber (2003) has developed a powerful alternative he calls *strong democracy*. In this highly collaborative form of decision making, he writes:

> The rightness of public acts depends then neither on a prepolitical notion of abstract right nor on a simple conception of popular will or popular consent. For what is crucial is not consent pure and simple but the active consent of participating citizens who have imaginatively reconstructed their own values as public norms through the process of identifying and empathizing with the values of others. (p. 137)

It is difficult to imagine how such a counter-hegemonic, democratic school community might be created when neoliberalism is the dominant ideology. However, this analysis makes clear that parents who advocate only for their own child within a school (advocating for ability-level tracking, for example) are often advocating for the neglect of the needs of other people's children. Barber's conception is useful in understanding the promise, but also the difficulty of creating counter-hegemonic spaces, those that aim to form a strongly inclusive and responsive democratic community when the hegemonic, or common-sense discourse, is that parents must be strong advocates for their own children, which contains elements of both good sense and bad sense.

These topics will be explored in greater depth, and in juxtaposition with the Mission Hill School approach, in Chapter 5.

Schools as Institutions of Control and Suppression

Activist and scholar Angela Davis (2003, 2005), among others,[5] has for many years been an outspoken critic of the enormous prison population in the United States, now numbering more than 2 million, a greater number of prisoners than any other country in the world, a disproportionate amount of whom are Black men. Davis refers to the prison industry, which involves rapacious forms of profiteering, as the prison-industrial complex. This cultural phenomenon is not entirely separate from the inequalities and suppression seen in U.S. schools today.

A growing number of scholars have shown how schools in the United States look and operate increasingly like prisons, and especially those schools serving low-income students of color (Anyon, 1997; Au, 2009; Johnson & Johnson, 2006; Kohn, 1999; Lipman, 2004; McNeil, 1986; Noguera, 2009). The word *suppression* refers to the ways in which the movement of children is strictly limited, orderliness and quiet are highly prized, children are often harshly punished for defying authority, the walls of schools are often barren, children are given few opportunities for play and decision making, and, rather than treating students like full human beings, the students' worth is too often reduced to test scores, with high-stakes decisions regarding the child's future as well as that of the teacher and school tied to them, creating pressure to narrow the curriculum and potential areas for intellectual growth. This situation has become a crisis of both inequality and of general suppression. It is unequal since poor children of color are disproportionately treated in this way, but it is problematic for children of all races, cultures, and socioeconomic situations and likely contributing to a growing dropout crisis (Orfield, Losen, Wald, & Swanson, 2004).

In order to understand the problem and to offer alternatives, it is also important to identify and acknowledge a theory of human learning and development. Even if all children were treated in this way it must be seen as a reprehensible form of suppression, violating Gutmann's principle of nonrepression. Suppressing children in the ways described above contradicts the best knowledge available about what children need to grow and develop, including intellectual and physical stimulation, attachment to reliable adults, fresh air, sunlight, exercise, nutrition, play, and a safe and accepting community (Bowlby, 1988, 2005; Chomsky, 2002; Dewey, 1938; Duckworth, 2007; Froebel, 2005; Gardner, 1983; Gee, 1996; hooks, 1994; Knoester, 2003, 2004; Kohn, 1999; McLaughlin, 2012; Meier, Engel, & Taylor, 2010; Piaget, 1973; Piaget & Inhelder, 2000; Vygotsky, 1978, 1986; Weber, 1997). Educators advocating a progressive view of learning build on the work of Froebel (2005) and Dewey (1900, 1902, 1916, 1938), among others, who argue children have their own internal needs that need to be met in order to grow and develop fully. A heavy set of top-down standards—whether tied to academic curricula or to behavior expectations and forced onto children through a system of rewards and punishments—denies a child's need to make decisions, to become the protagonist in their own lives, and to become effective democratic citizens. Dewey (1900) memorably wrote that

> the child is the starting point, the center, and the end. His development, his growth, is the ideal. It alone furnishes the standard. To the growth of the child all studies are subservient; they are instruments valued as they serve the needs of growth. Personality, character, is more than subject matter. Not knowledge or information,

but self-realization is the goal. To possess all the world of knowledge and lose one's own self is as awful a fate in education as in religion. Moreover, subject matter never can be got into the child from without. Learning is active. It involves reaching out of the mind. It involves organic assimilation starting from within. (p. 9)

Dewey refers here to children's growth as *the standard* and insists they not be seen through a *deficit* lens, or, in Locke's term, as a tabula rasa, or blank slate. Instead, children learn best when they are actively engaged and their curiosity is aroused. When Dewey writes, "subject matter never can be got into the child from without" the implicit assumption is that students are active agents of learning with the mental ability to make key decisions in their own education.

Other figures often cited by progressive educators for their contributions to a progressive theory of learning include Piaget (1941, 1973) and Duckworth (2007), who theorized natural stages through which children develop based on genetics and environmental stimulation and experience; Gardner (1983), who built on the work of Chomsky (1980) and Fodor (1982), among others, to profoundly trouble the notion of a single "intelligence" that can be quantified or compared with others, arguing that the mind is highly modular and teachers and educational settings should value the multiple intelligences of children; and Freire (1970), who developed an influential pedagogy of teaching literacy not only in the traditional meaning of the word, but literacy for critical consciousness and political empowerment, using a pedagogy that challenged the traditional hierarchy between the teacher and the student.

What each of these progressive educators have in common is a critique of the notion that knowledge can be merely passed on to learners in a top-down, controlling manner to docile students. Rather, human nature and learning must be seen as much more complex and active; students must be active participants in both the *learning* of knowledge and in its *creation*. Students must be seen as agents in history and in their own learning; and a more democratic approach, which respects the abilities and knowledge of students, will ultimately create a more just and democratic learning environment.[6]

It is a political stance for schools and educators to consciously attempt to stimulate the curiosity of students and allow students to make decisions, and mistakes, even as this may be at the expense of the appearance of orderliness and docility, and as a large chorus of school observers—including those critics on the left who also decry the inequalities of resources among schools—charge that schools should cover ever more material, especially for students from marginalized or oppressed groups. A school like Mission Hill, described in these pages, is organized to produce graduates who will not simply follow orders but will be feisty members of a democratic community, weigh evidence and use wise judgment, and be willing to take a stand and argue forcefully for what they believe is right.

I do not wish to be misunderstood here. I am not arguing that particular bodies of knowledge are not important for children to master in order to access discourses of power in society or to become effective citizens in a democracy. However, in order to teach powerful sets of knowledge, skills, and dispositions, educators must also be students of human nature and how children learn, all while valuing the unique personhood of children, as children are also capable of strongly resisting forms of education or relationships they interpret as disrespectful to their personhood (Dance, 2002; Kohl, 1995).

One aspect of these considerations is valuing the long-term effects of educational interventions, including the identity development of children and the formation of habits of the mind—for example, the habit of asking from whose perspective a story is told and evaluating the validity of evidence in an argument—rather than placing a high premium on specific knowledge that might be utilized for short-term gains on test scores, but is quickly forgotten. Highly valuing particular pieces of information for a test often requires pedagogical approaches that, for young children, can harm the development of longer-term educational goals (Ayers, 2004; Dance, 2002; Gee, 1996; Knoester, 2009; Meier, 2002; Meier & Wood, 2004; Noguera, 2003).

I will describe and discuss these topics in more depth in Chapter 6, and I will show how the Mission Hill School approaches curricula in light of this critique of the hegemonic belief in the need to control and suppress children.

Schools' Reliance on a Reductionist View of Students

As numerous scholars have argued, relying on standardized test scores as indicators of educational success or failure is laden with reductionism and fallibility (Au, 2008; Kohn, 1999; Koretz, 2009; McNeil, 2000; Meier, 2002; Meier & Wood, 2004; Sacks, 1999). They have shown that standardized tests do not reliably measure student learning but are instead strongly correlated with the income levels of students' families, among other social factors. In addition, it is difficult to determine how comparisons of test scores and other measures of academic achievement are helpful to democratic education or education for democratic citizenship. For example, the measure used by test makers to decide which children are "proficient" are not transparent or decided based on broad democratic deliberation. Standardized tests are generally created by for-profit corporations and are not aligned with the mission statement of individual schools, such as that of the Mission Hill School. Further, due to the increasing burden on schools to raise test scores, pressure is placed on teachers and schools to ignore the mission statements of their schools and the needs of individual children based on professional judgment, and instead to cut the items from the curriculum that do not contribute directly to the short-term gain of raising standardized test scores—a decision which may have harmful long-term effects on students.

There are far better alternatives to this method of assessment. Examples of formative assessments, or those assessments used by teachers to guide teaching practices, include the use of descriptive reviews, running records, performance assessments, discussions with parents and colleagues, and close observations of children in various settings and circumstances. And in terms of summative assessments, or those that take place at the end of a learning period and are more useful in judging teachers and schools, a set of assessments are necessary, such as a portfolio of student work, a public presentation, and a school-based, timed test or oral examination (Carini, 2001; Carini & Himley, 2010; Clay, 2000; Darling-Hammond & Ancess, 1994; Engel, 2005; Himley, 2000; Lyne, 2005; Meier, 1995, 2002; Peters, 2000).

These topics will be discussed in much more detail, as they relate to Mission Hill School practices, in Chapter 7.

Schools' Failure to Value the Importance of Teachers to Student Learning

Gutmann (1999) argues that the teaching profession suffers from an ossification of office, which inhibits teachers' ability to educate for democratic citizenship (p. 77; Apple, 2006; Cooper & Sureau, 2008; Kahlenberg, 2006). Due to perennially low salaries, inadequate working conditions, low status, increasing work intensification, and lack of decision-making power, approximately 50% of new teachers leave the teaching profession before they complete their first 5 years of teaching (Cochran-Smith, 2006; Ingersoll, 1995, 2003; Johnson et al., 2004). This is a troubling finding, since studies have repeatedly shown that staffing schools with high-quality teachers is the factor that matters *most* in attempts to improve schools, a project made considerably more difficult with a high rate of teacher turnover, and a problem affecting urban schools hardest (Darling-Hammond, 1997b, 2010; Ingersoll, 1995; National Commission on Teaching and America's Future, 2007).

At the center of teaching and learning is a relationship and an apprenticeship between the teacher and the student. Unfortunately, teachers are often at the margins of decision making in and about schools. Apple (1988, 1995) has described how scripted curricula and the dominance of assessment-driven teacher evaluations are leading to the deskilling of teachers, with detrimental effects on student learning. He also suggests that the history of teaching as a gendered occupation—largely female, while administrators have generally been male—has contributed to these effects.

An alternative and more sound approach to the lack of trust in the judgment of teachers to assess student learning, design curriculum, and make important decisions for the school is to instead invest in the knowledge of teachers; provide teachers with the time and support needed to be critically reflective practitioners and to continue to grow in their knowledge about curricular content, human development, and assessment (Cochran-Smith & Lytle, 1993, 2009; Darling-Hammond, 1997a, 1997b; Hawkins, 1974; Zeichner, 2009). Since the central relationship at the heart of teaching and learning in school is between the teacher and the student, it must be through the investment in teacher knowledge and through the political stance of empowering teachers with decision-making capacity that this process can be improved (Darling-Hammond, 1997b, 2010; Gee, 2004; Hawkins, 1974; Knoester, 2011a).

I will return to these topics in Chapter 8, where I present a description and analysis of how the Mission Hill School approaches the matter of teacher autonomy and professional development.

CONCLUSION

A school that hopes to be democratically inclusive and responsive and to help students develop the habits of mind necessary for effective democratic participation must be aware and thoughtful about the powerful forces of inequality and suppression that affect their ability to provide their students with an effective education. They must continually strategize and find ways to counteract these forces, which are rooted in capitalism, racism, and patriarchy and dehumanize the people that attend and work in schools. Without a plan of action for counteracting these forces, schools can come to embody the five traits of undemocratic schools described above: insensitive and disrespectful to the constituencies they serve, unresponsive to the desires of parents (especially working-class parents of color), heavily focused on control and suppression, overly reliant on reductionist assessment practices, and neglecting the central relationship at the heart of schooling—that is, the relationship between the teacher and the student.

In the pages that follow I describe how the Mission Hill School has intentionally and deliberately put in place practices that intend to be inclusive and responsive to the constituencies it serves, to counteract the forces of inequality working within schools, as well as point to the tensions and problems that remain or emerge in the process.

3

The Politics and Practical Challenges of Opening a New School

Instead of castigating and decrying their failures, and inadvertently joining the chorus clamoring for their total demolition, those who recognize the value and the importance of the services schools provide must instead adopt a position of critical support. In the same way that it would be unwise for criticisms of over-crowded buses or trains to prompt calls to abandon mass transportation, those who deplore conditions in urban public schools must recognize that, despite their weaknesses, urban public schools are desperately needed by those they serve.

–Pedro Noguera, *City Schools and the American Dream*, p. 7

THE NEIGHBORHOOD

Since I live just a few blocks from the Mission Hill School, I am, unfortunately, too often lulled into waiting until the last minute to walk to school. I start working on school-related planning early each morning, but I am often the last person to arrive at morning staff meetings. It's a frequent observation among some staff members—the students and colleagues who live closest to the school building seem to be the last to arrive. There is a reasonable explanation: those who drive must plan extra time for the unpredictable Boston traffic. I thought about this problem as I briskly walked through the neighborhood, across the parking lot of the community college, and to the bridge over rumbling trains, toward school. I pass under the shadow of the handsome 19th-century standpipe built on Fort Hill, named for the Revolutionary-era earthen fort that once overlooked this first southern suburb of Boston. History and urban development and decay surround my neighborhood and that of the school. As I walk from Fort Hill to Mission Hill I pass an empty brick building, a remnant of Roxbury's past as a center for beer making in the United States. Twenty-four breweries once thrived in these environs, before Prohibition put most of them out of business forever. I pick up my pace over cracked pavement and by weed lots as I try not to be the last person to the meeting again. A train rattles by, a reminder of the neighborhood battle that prevented a highway from being built for distant commuters at the expense of entire neighborhoods, rather than this subway that serves locals. I hike up the hill past two- and three-story clapboard houses and a community garden where the school maintains a plot. I notice winter squash ready to be picked. I arrive at the school—a three-story blond brick building with green window frames. I am panting but not the last one to arrive.

In Chapter 2 I described the theoretical framework I used to analyze and contextualize the data in this study. In this chapter I describe how the Mission Hill School came into existence—the political circumstances that allowed for a new school to open in Boston, why Deborah Meier decided to submit a Request for Proposal to the Boston Public Schools to open a new pilot school, some of the first decisions that were made, how the first staff members were hired, how parents became aware of the new school, and how staff dealt with some of the challenges they faced in the first year after the school's opening.

THE ORIGINS OF MISSION HILL SCHOOL

Particular political realities allow new schools to open. At least three major forces converged in the late 1990s that created the possibility for Mission Hill School's opening. The first was the creation of a new kind of school in Boston, called pilot schools. Pilot schools in Boston are regular public schools; they receive the same funding, from the same sources, as all Boston Public Schools; pilot school teachers are members of the Boston Teachers Union (BTU) and the Superintendent of the Boston Public Schools (BPS) is also the superintendent of pilot schools. The first pilot schools were opened in 1995 as a new model of school, meant, in part, to increase the choices available for parents within the Boston Public Schools system. Compared to non-pilot BPS schools, pilot schools are granted substantially more control over the following:

1. How their budget is used (Pilot schools receive their budget in a lump sum based on enrollment.)
2. Who they hire and keep as teachers (Pilot schools may hire outside of the pool of permanent BPS teachers except in the case of teacher layoffs due to budget shortfalls.)
3. What curricula will be used (Pilot schools must administer state exams but may administer separate curricula from their counterparts.)

4. How the school is governed (Pilot schools may organize governing bodies such as governing boards to hire and fire the principal, for example.)
5. How the school calendar and schedule will be the same or different from all Boston schools (Pilot schools may close school or open school on days the BPS calendar does the opposite, for example.) (Center for Collaborative Education 2006a; Knoester, 2011a)[1]

Pilot schools are different from charter schools, however, in that they are part of the Boston Public School system, teachers are members of the Boston Teachers Union, students at the school must be residents of the city, and pilot schools receive their funding from the city. This contrasts with charter schools, which generally receive their funding from the state, do not require students to live in a particular geographic area, and generally employ non-unionized teachers (Knoester, 2011a).

The second force that allowed the Mission Hill School to open is that in 1996 the BPS was planning, and had negotiated with the Boston Teachers Union, to open several new pilot schools, and put out a call for Request for Proposals (applications) for new pilot schools.

The third force that allowed Mission Hill School to open is that Deborah Meier, someone with a considerable reputation for leading successful urban schools, having helped to found and lead four well-known schools in New York City, was at just this moment strongly considering the possibility of once more opening a new school, this time in Boston. Meier recounted the story to me in an interview:

[In 1996] I was working with Annenberg [Foundation] . . . but . . . I really wished I was back in a school. The thought occurred to me that maybe I should just start a new school and maybe it should be in Boston where I wouldn't get back into being in the middle of the politics of schooling [in New York] and I had more freedom . . . and that I would be able to reconnect with a number of very close friends that I had for many years and who lived in Boston. I don't know if I knew about pilot schools, I think I found out about them when I was up there . . . I ran into . . . Bob Pearlman [a Vice President of the Boston Teachers Union] on the street and he told me about them, and then Vito Perone [a friend and Harvard Professor] said, "Why don't you call up Payzant [the superintendent of the Boston Public Schools]?" And I knew Payzant, we were both [founding board members] on the National Board for Professional Teaching Standards together, and had gotten friendly, so, all these parts fell together.

I asked Meier directly what had made the Mission Hill School possible, and this was her reply:

> Well, probably the fact that the pilots [existed]. . . . And probably the fact that [Superintendent] Payzant more or less trusted me, was a help. And also, that I had a good relationship with the unions, the teachers union in New York, so, you know, since they [the Boston Teachers Union] were part of the selection of schools, that probably helped.

Because all of these forces converged, there were perhaps fewer political obstacles to surmount in opening this new school, as compared with many other new schools. Brenda Engel, for example, one of the friends who supported Meier's desire to open a new school in Boston, had been intimately involved with opening another school previously, in Cambridge, Massachusetts. Engel characterized the political differences between opening Mission Hill School and her previous school in Cambridge:

> In Cambridge we met and planned for the school we wanted for years. We talked to all of the people in the neighborhoods, and convinced parents and taxpayers and the school committee to support the school. It was politically very difficult. For Mission Hill, Debbie dealt with the politics, and she had power, with Harvard and Vito. She went in holding a lot of cards. So it was in that way different. We [in Cambridge] didn't have power, we had an idea.

When the Request for Proposal for the Mission Hill School was accepted, Meier was brought by a BPS official to an empty former parochial school building in the Roxbury section of Boston, which had been acquired from the Catholic Diocese by the Boston Public Schools for the purpose of opening two new pilot schools. The three-story building would be housing three institutions starting in the fall of 1997: a small pilot high school on the third floor, the Mission Hill (K–8) School on the second;[2] and additional office space, a library, and a nonprofit curriculum development organization on the first floor. It immediately became apparent that many steps would need to take place before the school could open. The fact that Meier and the founding organizing group named above faced fewer obstacles than many in opening a school had many advantages. But one disadvantage, and a factor about which Meier was keenly aware, was that the school still had to start from scratch, and in a short amount of time, had to gain support and commitment from staff, prospective parents, and community members.

Staff Recruitment and Beginnings of Building a Democratic School Culture

Meier and Engel began distributing flyers about the school and holding informational meetings in various locations around Roxbury. And they needed to hire staff. The first person hired was an African American teacher and administrator at the Cambridgeport School, Brian Straughter. Straughter had heard of Meier's plan to start a new school and introduced himself at one of the many informational meetings Meier and Engel held for prospective parents. After Meier called the Cambridgeport School and received rave reviews about Straughter, he was soon hired and started meeting with Meier, Engel, and other planners at Engel's house. I asked Straughter what he remembered about those first meetings in the spring of 1997:

> I remember having soup at Brenda's house. . . . We had our Friday meetings at Brenda Engel's house and, we would be there for hours and Brenda would make soup. . . . I was very charmed by getting together, getting to know people . . . going out and visiting the next person who would be hired . . . and we were all full-time at our individual schools. . . . I remember feeling like we had two full-time jobs then.

Before anyone was hired, it was clear that Meier and her original working group had decided, and articulated in the Request for Proposal, that the school was to be a highly democratic, staff-governed school, a possibility, given the autonomies granted to pilot schools. Straughter recalled how that impacted their original hiring decisions:

> [We] talked about being a staff-governed school and figuring out how to articulate that to other potential people that joined the staff. And when we brought people on we thought they needed to be very strong teachers, but they also had to be people we really could get along with because we were going to spend so much time together.

Geralyn Bywater McLaughlin was another one of the first teachers hired before the school opened, to fill one of the two combined kindergarten and 1st-grade classrooms. Previous to this she had taught for 11 years at a progressive private school in Chestnut Hill, Massachusetts. She recalled some of the original planning meetings that were held at the Boston Children's Museum, before the school building was cleaned and prepared for opening:

One [teacher at another school] asked me, "What's it like, working for Debbie Meier?" And even in those early weeks that question struck me as being the wrong question. And, I said, "I don't work for Debbie Meier. I work *with* Debbie Meier." And, so, I can't remember, honestly, what we were deciding, I just remember feeling like I was part of the decision making. So, even though Debbie had strong opinions from the beginning, we were all doing it together.

Chapters 4 and 5 will describe in more depth the culture and processes of shared decision making at Mission Hill. However, at this point it is worth mentioning that in almost all of the interviews I conducted with staff and parents to learn more about their experiences with the school, Meier's sometimes forceful and intense personality was mentioned, along with Meier's insistence on shared decision making.

Heidi Lyne was the second teacher hired, and she started out as one of the teachers for the two 7-to-9-year-old classrooms. Lyne remembered:

It was trial by fire, in some ways. Deborah argued forcefully. But we came out so much stronger and better. It worked, by pushing us to take ownership, and to have a voice. We would go to informational meetings and Deborah would say to Brian and me, "You answer questions."

James McGovern was another teacher hired that first year, but only after one of the original five teachers left the school in its first semester. McGovern had an interesting educational history. He had grown up working class, going to public schools. He also had a forceful and charismatic personality (he soon proved himself able to hold his own in arguments even with Meier). He had attended and taught at progressive (public) schools his entire life, including attending as a child the school Brenda Engel helped to start in Cambridge. McGovern was also a colleague of Brian Straughter at the Cambridgeport School just before being hired at Mission Hill. McGovern had interviewed, along with Straughter, for a position before the Mission Hill School opened. He was not offered that position, but when one of the original staff members left, he received a call from Straughter. McGovern recalled:

Brian called in late November, and said that they had had trouble keeping the teacher in the 4/5 [9- to 11-year-old classroom] and that it was a fairly tough group and was I interested in taking it? He felt like I could handle them and they needed someone who understood city kids and could really set them straight. So, I was flattered by that. Then Deb called me the next day and we immediately had a fight. And

I told her to stick her job. And she called me back 45 minutes later and apologized and said, "We've gotten off on the wrong foot," and that wasn't how she wanted things to go, and she realized that maybe she had been a bit hasty. And I said, "Well, fine. If you're willing to say that, I'll come in and we'll see how it goes." So, then, you know the rest of the story pretty much. How many times did Deb and I fight my first year? It was almost a weekly thing. It was being forged in a furnace, but I wouldn't trade that for anything. I enjoyed the confrontational nature of that relationship, although she was so much better at it than I was . . . I was basically studying at the feet of a master. But that was good, because I needed it. And she had told me on the phone I shouldn't expect a mentor. Because I had said, "I'm really interested in learning from you and learning what you know." And she said, "I'm not very good at mentoring. I'm not that kind of person." And, you know, she was wrong. I know what she meant. She meant that she's not all warm and fuzzy and she doesn't cater to your feelings and whatnot . . . but she taught me to pause and think. She taught me that everything matters, that every decision we make needs to be about the educational interests of our students, that there needs to be an explanation and a rationale, that you have to be willing to look in the mirror, and say, "Why am I doing this?" So I learned more from her than I have from almost any other adult that I can think of in my life.

Development of a Philosophy and the Mission Statement

Before Heidi Lyne, one of the original teachers at Mission Hill, was hired she was known by Brenda Engel, whose granddaughter was once in Lyne's class at a private progressive school in Cambridge, the Atrium, another relatively new school that Lyne had helped to found. Lyne recalls first seeing the building that would house the Mission Hill School:

I will never forget going to the school for first time. It was in April of 1997—with Brenda, Beth [a friend of Brenda's and former principal of a school in England], and Deb. The school was old and dusty. The doors were locked. I remember sitting and talking in what is now the library. It was an amazing room, even then. It was so exciting, I couldn't believe it.

Much of the way that Mission Hill School would be organized was similar to that of the Atrium School, so it is perhaps not surprising that Meier hired two of the original five teachers from that school, Lyne and Emily Gasoi. Both the Mission Hill School and the Atrium were very small schools

(Mission Hill started with just 100 students in grades K–5, and added a grade each year up to the 8th). In both schools teachers stayed with the same students for 2 years, so teachers could know both the students and their families well. In both schools the whole school came together each Friday to sing and share part of the work they were doing that week in their classes. Both schools had long and broad schoolwide interdisciplinary themes.

One difference between the two schools was that the Atrium was a private school educating largely middle- and upper-class White students. Mission Hill was to be a public school in which, like the previous schools Meier helped to found in New York, a majority of students were African-American, and over half qualified for free or reduced lunch, a proxy measurement for students from working-class or poor families. Lyne was clearly excited about working for such a school, but she also expressed concerns:

> Progressive education for privileged kids is relatively easy. I am less worried that kids are going to slip through the cracks. So one struggle was how to "tighten up" assessment and intervention, so for kids that are not going to learn in this way naturally . . . that we do not "lose" a single one of them. Real progressive education is very structured and very thoughtful. But at Mission Hill I felt like the stakes were higher.

Gasoi recalled how many of the staff planning meetings that first year included discussions about the mission statement of the school, with underlying progressive principles:

> We talked about [the mission statement] a lot, how long it should be, what values we wanted to emphasize . . . that we wanted to focus on values rather than skills. I think Heidi and Geralyn and I had a hand in drafting it, and then Deb and Brenda would go over it and we would present it at meetings and tinkered with it a lot. Adding, taking things out, arguing over emphasis. It was a real process.
>
> There is an underlying understanding about pedagogy [in the statement]. Mission Hill School pedagogy is based on Piagetian research on child development and learning, Constructivism—human beings construct their own understandings. This involves a lot of "playing," tinkering, puzzling, because one has to "upset" one's current understanding to be able to move to a new understanding. So you can see how project based, integrated, and contexualized curriculum would be very central to this kind of understanding of learning.
>
> Then there is Deweyan philosophy of the purpose of education. Schools are for socializing students to be engaged, informed, and

responsible citizens. School should emulate workshops where people work things out, intellectually and socially . . . learning skills comes through those more fundamental (and some would argue, more intrinsically compelling) life skills.

Recruiting Parents

Parents of children in the Boston Public Schools choose to send their children to a particular school based on a controlled choice program that involves selecting top preferences. When the Mission Hill School was opened it was not guaranteed a student body, so families had to be recruited. The founding administrators and teachers of the school therefore advertised the school around the neighborhood and held informational sessions about the school in the new school building, as well as in other places where people could gather.

Amina Michel-Lord is someone who began her relationship with the school as a parent and then joined the staff as an assistant teacher. She related her memory of attending one of the first informational meetings about the Mission Hill School and why she chose to send her daughter to the school the year it opened:

> I remember some chairs were in a circle in the library [of the new school]. And Deb talked about . . . multi-aged [classrooms], whole language, small, two adults in each room, maybe the individuality of the learning . . . and those things spoke to me. She probably talked about Central Park East, which helped relieve my [doubts about], "You know, they're kind of new . . . " I remember saying, "I don't want [my daughter] to be a guinea pig while people were trying to figure out this whole new school thing." And Debbie must have convinced me at that meeting that she knew what she was doing and I didn't have to worry too much that [my daughter] was going to be a science experiment.
>
> And then we got picked [in the lottery], and she showed up that first year, and the chairs and tables hadn't come in.

THE PRACTICAL CHALLENGES OF OPENING A NEW SCHOOL

Ordering Supplies

Michel-Lord alluded above to one problem the school faced as it opened— the furniture the staff ordered had not yet arrived. McLaughlin describes below some of the challenges involved in those original planning meetings before the school opened (and before knowing the supplies they ordered would be late), mentioning some of the support they received from other pilot schools:

> We also went over to talk with Dawn Lewis. She was the principal at Young Achievers [another pilot school], which was just down the street at that time, and did a lot of ordering with her, of materials. That was really hard . . . we got really upset with each other and angry, just . . . deciding on . . . blocks, and manipulatives, and, you know, smaller things, but millions of smaller things. And so many stupid forms to fill in . . . that was not easy.

Building Maintenance

I asked Straughter, who was originally hired as a teacher, but instead became an assistant principal of the school that first year, about his view of the greatest challenges the school faced the year it opened. This is how he replied:

> It was an old parochial building that had all kinds of problems, while it was a pretty beautiful structure, the bathrooms and the plumbing . . . and just stuff had to continually be done to keep it up.

Maintaining a building in a large public school system necessarily involved "working the system" of bureaucracy to receive necessary materials or renovations. Straughter continued:

> It was very, very different [from my previous school in Cambridge]. I mean, Cambridge only has fourteen schools in total . . . up until high school, there's only about fourteen, so it's a fairly small school district. Boston is a subway ride downtown.

Working with the City to Receive a Budget

Straughter noted that securing money for the school as an ongoing challenge, as well as defending the autonomies inherent with pilot school status. He explained:

> We [had] a budget allocation [that] went down one day by $5,000. And you can't . . . if they give you your allocation it should never go down. But one day it went down five grand and I called the budget director and said, "I noticed in our budget the allocation went down five grand." And the guy's response was, "Oh, you noticed that." I said, "Yeah, I did." He said, "Honestly, most people don't notice that."

What they do is they go in and after 4 years going . . . they realize they need a little money and they start going into schools and take money from the schools and most people don't notice. So I noticed and the next day I had my five grand back. You know immediately they want to avoid a headache and they just do it. But in terms of, you know, the curriculum, the superintendent for curriculum would tell us that we need to be following a certain program and I would push back and say we're not doing it because of the pilot autonomy . . . and I wouldn't back down because I really felt that you've got to stand up for what you believe is right. If you don't believe it's right then it's hard to fight it, but if you really believe it's right, ultimately you still might lose, but go down fighting. And the Superintendent would side with us and say, "You know, that's their right. This is what [pilot schools are] supposed to be trying to do."

Several parents remarked about the fact that there wasn't a playground anywhere on the premises, since the school was formerly a high school. One parent that first year said, "I think maybe I wanted the school yard to be a little bit different. But I knew that would come in time," so there were clearly physical challenges that first year of the school.

Articulating the School's Philosophy to Parents

Another one of the challenges that first year was showing and explaining to parents what was meant by progressive education, since many parents had had little to no experience with such schools. Straughter explained:

Some families in Boston were looking for something new, something different, [and they] just heard about Boston pilot schools . . . [they] looked at Mission Hill as something new, so it has to be better, and then when they got there it was seen as a foreign concept, because there's nothing like Mission Hill in Boston. Mission Hill pushes the envelope in terms of traditional education, and for many families in Boston, thinking of the demographics, there was culture shock, you know, "It's different from where I grew up." So families were like, "This is what you meant?" or "This isn't what I thought I was getting into." Other parents would try to help them understand more about what we were trying to do, trying to get the old buy-in, after families were here.

The challenge of communicating a unique educational vision to families who are accustomed to a more traditional approach is an important topic to which we will return in the chapters to come.

CONCLUSION

Opening a new school is never easy. Even when a school is led by a highly experienced staff, the challenge of securing appropriate space, qualified staff, and parents to buy in to the educational philosophy of the school can be overwhelming. The Mission Hill School faced many obstacles, but was able to forge a path and a mission that has sustained them for many years to come. In this chapter I touched on several of the steps that had to be taken to open this school, including hiring staff, recruiting parents, ordering supplies, writing and communicating the mission statement of the school, renovating an old school building, and working with the central public school office to receive a budget for essential items. Of course, these challenges were above and beyond the central task of creating a culture of learning among a group of students who were new to the school, a topic to which we will return. Although just a brief overview, this chapter offered a glimpse at how difficult it is to open a new school, even with the political support necessary for the school to open. The groundwork for the school was laid during this first year, and the selection of staff and parents who were committed—or at least open at this point—to the goal of education for democratic citizenship, was crucial. Articulation and deliberation around those goals took substantial time and effort, and it is clear from this overview of that year that many obstacles had to be overcome.

Before turning to a more in-depth discussion about curriculum at Mission Hill, in Chapters 4 and 5 I will describe the ways that Mission Hill School has been deliberate about creating an inclusive and responsive community, first by focusing on the demographic makeup of the school and how the staff and community has valued and thought about diversity and instituted social and curricular activities to build community and trust across cultural and social divisions.

4

The Promise and Challenges of Cultural Integration in a School

Democracy is not an alternative to other principles of associated life. It is the idea of community itself . . . a name for a life of free and enriching communion

John Dewey, *The Public and Its Problems*, p. 148

A FAMILY NIGHT AS IT UNFOLDS

Family nights at Mission Hill School generally begin with a time of mingling between faculty and families in the lobby of the school. It is a time for chatting with both the families of students in my classroom and those of former students, but also many others. In such a small school, it is not hard to know nearly everyone, and it is wonderful to see such a culturally diverse gathering of adults and children in one space. Children are often the topic of conversation, but in a much less formal way than at family conferences. I hear a story about one of my former students, now in high school. I learn more about the busy lives of children and adults. Parents enter carrying food from a diversity of cultural traditions—tin-foil-wrapped taco salad, Jell-O, rice and beans, and finger foods of many kinds—and place the dishes on folding tables lining the walls. Children do not hesitate to help themselves to the food right away so they can play in the library and down the hall with friends. As with most social events, Family Nights at Mission Hill School are planned before the "guests" arrive, and once the families arrive and eating begins, the plans unfold. I try to relax at the beginning of these gatherings, confident that the curricular presentations will go well, but always somewhat nervous. After a half hour of mingling and eating there is a loud whistle and my colleague, Heidi, who is standing on a chair, shouts, "Excuse me!" People quiet down and listen to her welcome message and encouragement to finish eating and to "Make your way upstairs to see what is going on in your child's classroom. But please make sure to come back down to the lobby for music by the Mission Hill Chorus at seven thirty."

Although Family Nights are generally informal events, I prepared for the evening by writing a greeting message on a board in front of the door. Students' work is displayed throughout the classroom and in the hallway outside. Many families have multiple children at the school, so they trickle in and out, moving from one room to another. If a large crowd of families enters at once I make a presentation summarizing what we have been working on and what is displayed throughout the room, but tonight, small groups of families enter with their children. I ask the students to explain to their families what we have been doing, and am happy to answer questions or add detail. The only tricky part is when parents want to continue conversations that began in the lobby that draw attention away from the student work. But it's a good problem to have—we enjoy each other's company, and there's so much to talk about. Deborah Meier and Brian Straughter pop in and are eager to greet each family. Suddenly, I can hear the school chorus singing "Lift Ev'ry Voice and Sing" downstairs, a shame, since I love their music and hate to miss any part of it. I walk with a parent back down the stairs, he hands me a book that he thinks I might enjoy and I am grateful.

In this chapter I focus on a crucial aspect of any school calling itself democratic—its inclusion of staff, parents, and students with cultural differences. I discuss in particular the demographics of the Mission Hill School and describe how various practices were put in place at Mission Hill to foster an integrated community, and describe how these practices were received by staff, parents, and students, as well as how tensions and challenges arose along the way.

THE PROBLEM OF SCHOOL SEGREGATION

The cultural segregation of schools is one of the most vexing problems in the history of U.S. education. According to a recent study:

> Schools in the United States are more [racially] segregated today than they have been in more than four decades. Millions of non-White students are locked into "dropout factory" high schools, where huge percentages do not graduate, and few are well prepared for college or a future in the US economy (Orfield, 2009, p. 1).

Boston school history is infamous for segregated schools. In the year 1974, Boston was the site of a desegregation court order mandating the busing of students between the largely Irish-American neighborhood of South Boston and the largely African-American neighborhood of Roxbury (Formisano, 2004; Hillson, 1977; Taylor, 1998). The program was met with resistance and, at times, violent protests.

In the years following the busing protests, a large majority of the European-American families sending their children to the Boston Public Schools (BPS) pulled them out of the schools and moved either to suburban neighborhoods or sent their children to parochial or private schools (Formisano, 2004; Hillson, 1977; Orfield & Eaton 1996; Taylor, 1998). The Boston "exam schools," highly selective high schools, with test-based admissions, became the only schools in the BPS with a majority European-American student population in a city that had, until recently, a majority European-American population (Center for Collaborative Education, 2006b; U. S. Census Bureau, 2008).

One recently retired Mission Hill School teacher, Roberta Logan, who spent more than 3 decades teaching in the Boston Public Schools, described the racial history of the BPS as "segregation, desegregation, and then resegregation."

THE DEMOGRAPHICS OF MISSION HILL SCHOOL

In light of this history, the Mission Hill School is remarkable for its rare example of integration. As I mentioned previously, the current demographics of the school are 41.4% Black, 27.8% Hispanic, 22.8% White, 0.6% Asian, and 7.4% mixed or "other." Elementary school averages in the Boston Public Schools are 33.7% Black, 12.6% White, 43.0% Hispanic, 8.3% Asian, and 2.3% "other" (Boston Public Schools, 2012; Massachusetts Department of Elementary and Secondary Education, 2012). These percentages, however, hide the fact that many of the White and Asian American students in the public system attend segregated Advanced Placement programs within segregated schools. In terms of income, 47.5% of Mission Hill School students qualify for federal free and reduced priced lunch, a proxy number for students from low-income families, while the BPS average for students who qualify for federal free and reduced-price lunch is 74.4% (Center for Collaborative Education, 2006b; Massachusetts Department of Elementary and Secondary Education, 2012).

This is an unusual demographic. These data suggest that Mission Hill School attracts a wealthier and Whiter group of families than the Boston Public School norm, but a more Black and Hispanic group of families than Advanced Placement programs in Boston or than the richer and Whiter suburban public and private schools in the Boston area.

The reasons for this integration are hard to pinpoint. Mission Hill School has been until recently a citywide school, which means that half of the student population could consist of students who live outside of the "walk zone." The location of the school is significant. It has been situated in a largely

Black and Hispanic neighborhood, but is near the border of a largely White and politically progressive district. Of course, with the mandated move of the school to a new neighborhood in the fall of 2012 this demographic may be difficult to sustain. Still, no other elementary school in the surrounding areas, or elsewhere in Boston, has achieved this kind of cultural integration. One explanation, espoused by several of the participants in my interviews, was that many of the Black and Hispanic students were drawn from the "walk zone," or the neighborhood directly surrounding Mission Hill, while many of the White students were bused to the school, and their parents may have heard about the work of Deborah Meier from her various writings and activities.[1] This would be an overstatement if it was taken to mean that many Black and Hispanic families had not also read or heard of Meier, or that many White families did not also live near the school and were attracted to Mission Hill for reasons other than the reputation of Meier.

Moreover, it should perhaps go without saying that my use of the term *integration* here is not reduced to merely a desegregated school, or a particular demographic makeup, as the demographics can change over time. It can be read on a number of levels. Research shows that cultural integration in schools is rare and difficult to achieve and to maintain (Kozol, 2005; Orfield, 2009). Even after court-ordered desegregation of schools, many schools continue to segregate within schools, with the use of tracking, for example (Conger, 2005).

BEING INTENTIONAL ABOUT INTEGRATION

From the year it opened, the founders of the Mission Hill School recognized that achieving and maintaining both a racially and culturally integrated school would be difficult, so immediately practices were put in place specifically to foster community, trust, and understanding, while more practices were added over time as challenges arose. For the remainder of this section I will outline and describe 12 key strategies or practices the school put in place to help foster a more integrated and welcoming community. Since these practices focus primarily on building community and trust among adults, this section will be followed by a focus on cultural integration and building community among students, a subject that will also be a topic in Chapter 6, focusing on curriculum.

Importance of Small Schools

First, opening Mission Hill School as a small school was intentional. Meier is a well-known advocate of small schools (Meier, 1995, 2002), and research has shown there are many benefits to small schools, among those is the possibility for people within the school to form relationships with every other person in the school (Ayers, Klonsky, & Lyon, 2000; Raywid, 1997, 1999, 2006). A parent I interviewed perhaps best summarized this aspect when she said:

> Two little things about the school totally impressed me when [my child] was there, and still impress me. One is the smallness, I love the smallness, but the other is, and I'm sure it's not every kid, but in general, when I go to that school . . . a kid who sees me is going to say "hello." If I say "hello" back, they're going to open the door for me as I'm walking up the stairs and I'm by the door. They're taught to be respectful and to have good manners. It's lovely. I mean, I've had the most wonderful experiences there, and her friends would talk to me, and friends of her friends, it was a lovely way of interacting.

The culture of caring described above cannot be attributed solely to the smallness of the school, of course, but the smallness makes it easier to create such a culture, a topic we will return to later in this chapter and in Chapter 6.

The Importance of a Culturally Diverse Staff

Another conscious decision on the part of Meier and the first staff members hired was to bring together a culturally diverse staff, in terms of race, class, and gender. This was important for many reasons. A diverse staff better reflects the diversity of the families sending their children to the school and allows staff to build a relationship with those families that allows people of all cultural groups to say to themselves, "This school is for people like me and belongs to people like me." If the school hired only White female staff, for example, which is often the case in schools across the country, parents and children of color are arguably more likely to conclude that the school does not "belong to, nor welcome, people like me."[2]

Hiring Parents for Staff Positions at the School

A third decision was to hire parents for various positions in the school. For example, the school office manager, the security guard, lunch and morning monitors, the school nurse, the school art teacher, and a variety of other job openings in the school went to parents of children in the school. It is not a coincidence that 1 year a full half of my 4th- and 5th-grade class had a parent working in the school. This sends many important messages to the community. On the one hand, staff who are parents bring to staff meetings important perspectives on being a parent, and on the other hand, they bring to parent meetings and gatherings the perspective of a staff person. Further, when parents enter the building and see a parent as a security guard (who does not wear a uniform or carry a weapon but does recognize every face that walks in the door), parents are more likely, again, to conclude that this school belongs to them. But it is a balance as well. As one founding teacher said to me, "You want parents to be involved in the life of the school, but you also want them to trust you as professionals to create a viable learning environment."

Avoiding Tracking and Ability-Grouping

A fourth conscious decision made by the school in the effort to integrate and be inclusive of its diverse population, was the refusal to track or rank students at the school. Even ability grouping is discouraged. These practices are found to create in-school segregation (Conger, 2005; Lipman, 1998; Noguera, 2003). Further, the staff at the school is discouraged from viewing or referring to only some children as "smart" and symbolizing this with awards or honor rolls, another topic I will return to in Chapter 6, where I will describe in more detail the curriculum and the progressive educational philosophy espoused by the school.

Religious Holidays are not Celebrated at the School

Fifth, the school does not celebrate religious holidays, birthdays, or use curricula that might be interpreted as exclusive of families' important values or beliefs. This does not mean that religious holidays are not discussed or recognized, but they are not *celebrated* in a way that is common in many schools. Celebrations at the school are common, but are generally reserved for accomplishments or events related to school-based themes or activities carefully chosen by the entire school and individual teachers to be inclusive and to have an educational purpose. A key part of the decision-making process about curricula is using what Ladson-Billings (1995) calls *culturally relevant pedagogy*, or planning curricula (hidden and overt) that sends a message to students and families that the school recognizes and values the diverse cultures that are brought to school (Ladson-Billings, 1995, 2006; Valenzuela, 1999). For example, the walls of the classrooms and hallways are decorated with student artwork, photographs, and posters intentionally reflecting cultural values and the school's diversity, including diversity of race and ethnicity, as well as of sexual orientation and religion. Part of the intention is for parents and students to notice when they enter the school that the school welcomes them and their culture. One Jewish parent, for example, reported to me in an interview the following:

> There was this one other quirky thing that might sound really benign, but given how I was brought up, I remember Deborah Meier explaining, because I asked her, "what holidays were observed in the school?" It was really important to me that the holidays were outside of the school environment, because as a Jewish child, I was brought up in a strictly non-Jewish town, and it was just incredibly hard for me, having to learn all the Christmas songs, and write about Christmas in Holland in social studies. I know it sounds like a quirky little thing, but it really . . . she won me over. I remember her telling me this and it made such sense to me.

Community Knowledge is Valued in the Curriculum

The sixth strategy, related to the fifth, is that the subject of study in the classrooms is often built around, and draws upon, community knowledge, geography, and institutions. For example, the first thematic unit the school staff designed in the year it opened was an exploration of the geography, people, and environment of the immediate neighborhood surrounding the school. As the years progressed, the school built strong and lasting partnerships with neighboring institutions, such as museums and universities (including two universities that send a steady stream of student teachers to the school), as well as businesses and nonprofit organizations, allowing interdisciplinary studies of history and architecture, business and the economy, mapping and geometry, and so on, to have relevancy and power for students, partly due to the close proximity of the objects of study, and to the personal relationships students built with neighbors.

Building Trust and Community with Shared Experiences in the School

Seventh, the school staff organizes a variety of gatherings designed to educate, as well as build community trust and bonding. Four prominent examples include: Friday Shares, monthly or bimonthly family nights, classroom performances, and beginning- and end-of-year cookouts. Friday Shares are weekly morning gatherings of the entire student body for approximately 30 to 45 minutes in the library. Parents are also encouraged to attend. The meetings begin and end with whole-group singing. The gatherings then feature the sharing of student work from four student representatives of four different classrooms. By the end of the school year every student has shared at least once to the entire school. As illustrated at the beginning of the chapter, family nights are potluck gatherings, which usually start in the lobby of the school, where parents, staff, and students eat and socialize, and then they move to classrooms where a variety of presentations, celebrations, or other activities take place, usually around a curricular theme. The beginning- and end-of-year cookouts are social in focus, and the classroom performances for parents and families are done on a more ad-hoc basis and are usually organized by individual teachers, while parents often help to plan and coordinate family nights and social gatherings. Referring to Friday Share, one parent remarked:

> We just liked it that the community came together on Friday Share once a week, instead of keeping everyone separate in their . . . you know, the 8th graders here and the kindergarteners here—that everybody was in the same room, feeling the same energy, and sort of seeing this is their community, visually, and acting in it.

Regarding the various family nights and potlucks, one parent remarked:

> There are so many potlucks and this and that, where you feel like it becomes a community, basically. You can only help but feel a part of it. You don't get a chance to feel separate. And I like that, because it means—and these are the potlucks, not the parent council—you smile when you come in here.

Another parent said this about one of the earliest family nights she remembers, from the first year the school opened, and before they became potlucks:

> Heidi would have families come in once a month, and just opened her classroom. I remember sitting in her room, where the adults were sitting at the table, and she ordered a couple of boxes of pizzas. The kids were off doing something. We were beading and just talking about school stuff, talking about kids, and I remember just feeling like . . . At [my previous school] you had family night, report cards, conferences, but this was so different, it was like Mission Hill was caring for us as a family. That sounds real corny, but it really was. I remember saying, "Wow, it's really awesome to hear other parents say they're struggling with their kids around food, or going to bed," or whatever it was . . . we were just sitting around talking about our kids.

Inclusive and Responsive Decision Making

Eighth, the governance of the school is highly democratic, in the sense that input from a wide range of voices is expected for making important decisions. While this factor helps to build community, it is a topic on which I will elaborate in much more detail in the following chapter, dedicated to shared decision making at the school.

Communicating Clearly and Effectively Between the Staff and Parents

Ninth, communication between the school and parents is taken very seriously, and is pursued in a variety of ways. When asked what she grew to like about the school over time, one parent specifically mentioned:

> I certainly appreciated their communication effort. You know, the real attempt to share what was going on—through the way they did their conferences, and the newsletters, and there was clearly a real effort being made to try to communicate.

This parent refers to the weekly newsletters sent home to families, reminding families of upcoming events, describing and showing (through photographs and narrative writing) the curricular focus of the school and individual classrooms through the use of a front page column, usually written by the principal and smaller columns written by each teacher, among other items in the newsletter. The newsletters, combined with formal narrative reports, family conferences, and more informal discussions, are the primary ways the school communicated with families, a topic to which I will return in Chapter 7.[3]

Addressing Difficult Issues Head-on and Schoolwide

Tenth, in an effort to address particular tensions among families and between families and the school staff that have arisen from time to time, a special set of discussions around race and culture were instituted, called *courageous conversations*. A professional facilitator was asked to lead the discussions, which were open to all families and staff. Important and sensitive issues relating to culture and schooling were raised and discussed in this setting, including feelings that certain people's voices were taken more seriously than others at family council meetings, while certain families were feeling marginalized.[4] There were also other deliberate attempts to talk about race community wide. Another event organized by the school to provoke discussions about race and gender among the adults in a safe space was a panel discussion of Black men, talking about their experiences as children and relating these experiences to the special tensions and challenges Black boys and their parents and families may be facing.

Building Trust and Community Among the Diverse Staff

Eleventh, the highly diverse staff also instituted several ways to create a trusting community among themselves. These include organizing regular staff retreats at remote getaway houses or retreat centers, where staff not only meet to plan for the school, but also enjoy one another's company while cooking and eating together, swimming in lakes, playing basketball, and other relaxing activities. One teacher, when asked what she appreciated about the school, replied:

> Hands down, what I really like are the people that I work with. On the good days, on the bad days, it always feels like a really tight-knit, cohesive, group of people that I can trust that I can, for the most part, rely on, and that we're all, you know, basically on the same page as far as how we want the school to run and what we want the kids to have.

Staff meetings at the school also often include food, sometimes paid for out of the school budget and sometimes provided by individual staff members on a rotational basis.

Creating a Comfortable and Informal Place to Be

And finally, the school has made a conscious effort to be a somewhat informal place for students, more like a home than an institution. Classrooms are furnished with comfortable chairs, couches, and beanbags; most classrooms have pets and plants; most adults—though not all—prefer to be called by their first names; and students often move around the classroom and school freely. One graduate recalled the first moment she transferred to the school:

> Yeah, just the way it looked, like there weren't any desks. There weren't any lockers. It was so small, and there were little kids around. And it was colorful, and there was artwork. And everybody seemed like—I don't want to say a hangout because we were learning and stuff—but it was in a very relaxed way.

I will return to this informal approach to the classroom and school in Chapter 6, as it is also a part of the curricular goal of counteracting the hidden curriculum found in many schools that sends messages to students that school is not for people "like me," for example. Part of the Mission Hill School pedagogy is to encourage a high degree of school ownership on the part of the students, tempered by an ongoing curriculum of showing respect and caring for others (Charney, 2002; Knoester, 2009; Paley, 1993).

BUILDING COMMUNITY AMONG STUDENTS

Community building is a critically important aspect of the educational approach of the school. Although these topics will be more seriously discussed in Chapter 6, it is worth mentioning here that each of the classrooms, and the staff more generally, plans and encourages fun and bonding experiences, especially outside of the school building, where students might form relationships that are perhaps less likely in the school building. These experiences include yearly trips to a farm run by visiting students and farm staff, called the Farm School, where students in 4th grade and older stay for 2 or more nights; classes take field trips to ice-skating rinks, museums, parks, and even to mountains for climbing; extracurricular opportunities include basketball, track, rowing, a robotics club, and a snowboarding club. In the school, weekly activities that foster student relationships across the grades include Friday Share, and a book-buddies arrangement, where 4th- and 5th-grade students read with kindergarten and 1st-grade buddies every Friday. Referring to the Farm School, one parent shared:

> [Our oldest child] used to say, "When people go to Farm School they get along even if they don't get along anywhere else." And so I do think that's really important.

In fact, every graduate I interviewed named experiences at the Farm School as among their favorite memories while at the Mission Hill School. And it is perhaps due to a combination of the above relationship-building practices that led one parent to say:

> You know, there are so many people in education . . . they don't know the kids, they don't really care. They say they care, and they don't. It's all lip service. These people really cared, and just for them to know [my children], and to know the struggles that they were under at that particular time anyway, it was amazing. It used to bring tears to my eyes when I would go in there, and they would care so much. Not just knowing their names, but knowing their lives, and knowing what they were going through in their struggles. It was quite the holistic approach to education, which I don't see anywhere else.

While each of these strategies of building trust and community are integral to what makes the Mission Hill School unique, I do not wish to paint a portrait of an idyllic setting where all educational or behavioral problems are solved through these means. At times, much heavier educational interventions are used to address various challenges, including gatherings of all family members, relevant teachers, and specialists to work closely with particular students around a particular question or problem. There are times, for example, when Herb Kohl's (1995) *I Won't Learn from You* describes well a form of resistance to schooling or to particular individuals that students are quite capable of demonstrating. It is precisely in these circumstances that a small, personal school makes possible the flexibility to marshal together the people or resources needed to make interventions around particular students, where all adults in the school can work together to create a place where a vulnerable student, for example, can thrive, another topic to which we will return in Chapter 6.

TENSIONS AND CHALLENGES IN CREATING A TRUST-BASED, INTEGRATED COMMUNITY

As suggested above, relations among cultural groups are not perfect at the Mission Hill School. In the eyes of some, they have been far from perfect. Several statements to this effect emerged in my interviews. Above all, parents and teachers were concerned about the demographics and dynamics of the Family Council meetings. The Family Council is a body made up of all of the parents, but the attendance at the meetings for several years did not reflect the demographics of the school. According to one parent, who happened to be Black, the Family Council could be characterized as

> overzealous White folks, who are really interested in knowing what's best, or believing they know what's best, and not seeking direction, support, insight from the constituents or the parents who can't make it to the meetings because they have to work. There's not a lot of outreach in the way that I think there should be, as far as, some of the folks on the parent council think sending an e-mail is enough, and/or a flyer. And quite frankly, lots of people don't have e-mail like that. The balance of the parent council, or the people who show up for parent council, does not match what the school looks like. I think there are some voices that get lost. And, to me, there's a slight demonization of those who don't make it to the meetings, based on this idea that they don't want to, as opposed to, they don't have time to. I know that we're thinking about it, but there's not a way that's effective yet to get the feedback, the concerns of parents who cannot or do not make it to the meetings. So it's sort of one type of concern. And, frankly, when I go to the meetings I don't want to be there because there's only one or

two or three people of color there, usually one. And if I'm there, two. And it's just not comfortable.

This sentiment was echoed by more than a few parents and staff members. The phenomenon of White middle-class parents having disproportionate voice in a racially diverse school has also been found and analyzed in research literature (Horvat, Weininger, & Lareau, 2003; Lareau & Horvat, 1999).[5] Various actions have been taken at the school to address this perceived imbalance. However, the following example illustrates the complexity of the politics of race and class at Mission Hill School. Early in the school's history parents began to form a group specifically for parents of students of color. But just as the group was forming at least one parent (of mixed race) was upset by the idea of this group, finding the idea of it to be more divisive than inclusionary. According to this parent:

> I remember speaking to one of the parents that was kind of leading this group. And they were meeting at the school. And I said, "Who are the parents of the children of color?" And they said, "Well, it's all the African Americans." And I said, "Well, I have children of color." And she was like, "Oh." And I said, "I'm [of mixed race]." And she said, "Well, okay." We talked. And she was like, "Well, if you want to come." Then soon after, I actually went and told them that I was going to call the superintendent if this group didn't stop meeting in school.
>
> There was a couple who had adopted a Black child. And they refused to let the parents in the group. . . . And I went to the assistant principal and I basically said, "If you don't do something I'm going to make noise. I'm going call the superintendent. That's illegal, that group." And it ended. If they want to go meet in someone's house, feel free. But they should not be doing this in school. And the reason I brought it up is my daughter is bringing home the flyer and she is asking, "Who is this? Which parents are invited?" So that was kind of a big deal to me, yeah.

We will return to this important topic in Chapter 5, as issues of decision making at the school are central. As we focus on tensions and dilemmas of a culturally diverse community in this section, issues of gender and sexual orientation also arise.

Gender and Sexual Orientation

Mission Hill School is a community with a substantial number of gay and lesbian staff and families, a group that is often marginalized in schools

(Blackburn, Clark, Kenney, & Smith, 2009). Several participants in my interviews made statements about how particular issues having to do with gay and lesbian members of the community could have been handled better by the school. One parent said the following in response to my question, "Does the school's view of social justice coincide with the views of your family?"

> [M]y disappointment was, as a gay parent, that when gay marriage came to Massachusetts that it was not noted by my child's teachers in any way, even though my child was very open that her parents were getting married, and in her way, why this wasn't important. To this day, although I think we both spoke out about it, it was usually upsetting to me in the same way that if it wasn't noted in Mission Hill now that Barack Obama is president and what that means for this country, if that was ignored. I just wouldn't understand it. To me, history in the making in a school is the time to help children. So that piece of gay rights that was missing at such a historic time in Massachusetts was not in keeping with our social understanding of social action, and justice. But in every other way I think it was. For me, I think it was.

Intolerance Among Students

Problems of acceptance were also reported by several of the graduates I interviewed. One student and his parent complained about the lack of acceptance of their religion at the school. Another graduate remembered being teased by other students even when she was going through a very difficult time in her life at home. One set of parents reported that there was a time when they tried to host a party for all of the children in the child's class and not a single person came to the party. Several parents speculated that the cultural gaps among students were so wide that even at a rather tight-knit community like the Mission Hill School it was very hard for some students to form bonds.

THE IMPORTANCE OF CULTURAL DIVERSITY

Cultural Diversity as a Key Reason for Choosing Mission Hill School Among Parents

Nevertheless, despite all of the tensions and struggles raised by various participants in our interviews, it is more than a little interesting to note that when I asked each parent and graduate whether they thought the cultural diversity at Mission Hill was an important reason for sending their child there, without exception, every parent said "Yes," and a large majority of graduates said they thought the diversity of the school positively contributed to their educational experience. Here is how one parent summarized her appreciation for integration:

> I want my kids to grow up loving everybody, learning about all different people, you know, so there'll be no racism, no bigotry . . . I think it's very important. I always try to get them in a school with a lot of different races, that they're not the minority, or the majority. That's one of the good things about this school, there are all kinds of races here. And I never see any kids in this school calling anybody out of their name for race, or anything, never. They all seem to get along. Oh yeah, that's very important to me. And my kids being mixed . . . them being biracial, half Black, half White, I want them to be comfortable in the schools they go to.

Another parent described an important benefit she believes her children received as a result of having been part of the diverse Mission Hill School community:

> My kids, all of my kids, especially the older girls, who went all the way through or went through the upper grades and went through a lot of social issues at Mission Hill, have very open . . . how can I say this? Their ability to deal with different people, races—it's very nice. So, it's interesting. And they struggled, you know. But there is an element of real compassion. So, it's interesting, very interesting.

One graduate reflected in this way on what she gained from attending a culturally integrated school:

> I went to Mission Hill for 6 years. And it was 170 kids when I was going there, so tiny. And . . . the similarity, the big similarity between Mission Hill and [her high school] is the gay community, it's huge. Huge. And that's probably one of the best things that could have happened to me, just because I come from a very homophobic family and—you can relate to people so much better. You're so much more open-minded to them.

The Importance of Affection and Strong Community Among Staff

Staff members also described the importance of being part of and helping to create a diverse and culturally integrated community, while also describing how challenging it can be, and that one aspect of creating a trusting community must be open communication about matters that can be hard to talk about. One staff member expressed her view in this way:

The relationships between adults at Mission Hill were just more authentic [compared to my previous school]. I had good working relationships with people at the [previous school], but we didn't hang out after work, our kids didn't hang out together. At Mission Hill we babysit each other's kids, the working relationships are just more genuine, more solid, more personal. And I think the reason why those personal relationships developed is because of the way we work together, which is why I feel like sometimes the retreats can be so difficult, because you're trying to hold everybody accountable for their working relationship, and sometimes that's hard because there is the personal, so if the working isn't going so great, how do you work that out? In personal relationships you want to make sure that everybody feels okay, so it kind of gets all mushy. It's one thing we're trying to work on now, you have to have those hard conversations.

The Low Number of Behavioral Incidences at the School

There is much more to be said about these topics—including the on-going tensions and the many other strategies, both successful and less so, that the staff and parents at Mission Hill School have used to address these issues. These conscious strategies to create an integrated and inclusive community are a major part of what makes the Mission Hill School unique and perhaps able to accomplish other elements of its mission, topics I will turn to in the following chapters. It is worth noting that the number of behavior incidents, such as suspensions and expulsions, at Mission Hill School are among the lowest in the Boston Public Schools. Students are very rarely suspended and never expelled (Boston Public Schools, 2012; Center for Collaborative Education, 2006b). Although it is impossible to pinpoint a precise reason for this fact, it is reasonable to conclude that the intentional and proactive efforts to build an integrated and inclusive community, although imperfect, likely play a major role in these successes.

CONCLUSION

Creating a culturally integrated and trusting school community is an elusive goal for most of the nation's schools. The Mission Hill School, a culturally diverse school, has examined these issues and has instituted particular strategies that aim to address the tensions that sometimes arise when diversity is present. Challenges continue to arise, but a democratic school must be committed to creating inclusive and responsive opportunities for students, which also means providing spaces for parents to be included in the life of the school, to form trusting relationships with staff and others at the school, and to provide means to deliberate on difficult issues to the benefit of the entire school.

In this chapter I identified the problem of school segregation in Boston and the demographics of the Mission Hill School, and described 12 specific strategies that the school community has practiced to foster an inclusive and integrated school community. If a school is focused on educating students for effective democratic citizenship, it helps for students to know and understand their own culture and the similarities and differences of people from other cultures. This is best done when students are learning together within a diverse group of peers and adults, where difficult discussions and explorations around race, gender, abilities, and class can be had. This is not always easy, but parents and graduates alike indicated that this is a crucial part of an education at Mission Hill School, and the school community took many deliberate steps to foster these kinds of rich exchanges.

We turn next to the topic of shared decision making at Mission Hill School, a key aspect to any school calling itself democratic.

5

Shared Decision Making at the School Level

Democratic schools, like democracy itself, do not happen by chance. They result from explicit attempts by educators to put in place arrangements and opportunities that will bring democracy to life.

–Michael Apple & James Beane, *Democratic Schools,* p. 9

A THOROUGH PRE-HIRE VETTING

Every teacher at the Mission Hill School has an interesting story to tell about how he or she was hired. The more I hear the stories of others, the more I realize how unique this experience was. It was, in a word, thorough, and not even comparable to the first time I was hired as a teacher, when the principal told me on the phone, "It's a go," without even an interview (although I had been a substitute teacher in the school for some time). When the Mission Hill School hired me as a "lead teacher" (after I had been an assistant teacher), they wanted to make sure that both they and I knew what we were getting into and to make clear to the entire school community that they were serious about shared decision making and careful deliberation about key decisions. My hiring consisted of six steps. The first step was to submit an application, cover letter, resume, and official transcripts. The next step was to visit the school, which was not a problem for me, since I had already worked as an assistant teacher at the school for several months by this time. Next, I was called and invited to teach a demonstration lesson. It is an intimidating thing to do, teaching a high-pressure lesson to students you don't know well, but teachers and parents lined the classroom walls while I taught, so I comforted myself by reasoning that the students would be on their best behavior with so many adults in the room (and they were). I remember I taught a reader's workshop lesson that began with a read-aloud, moved to a discussion about the content and language of the book, and then I asked students to write their own stories, keeping our discussion in mind. It ended with the group coming back together and sharing what they wrote. It must have gone well, because after the demonstration lesson I was invited to interview with the hiring committee. I sat at a large table and was questioned by six people, including staff members, parents, and students. Behind them were several rows of folding chairs set up for other staff members and parents to listen and observe. There were approximately 12 such observers during my interview. That was the fourth step. Next, Deborah Meier called all of my references, and then called me to further press me on questions that arose during those conversations that she wanted to know about, since she was present, but not at the table for the formal interview. And last, I was asked to return to the school to answer more follow-up questions with three other staff members who did not have a chance to be at the questioning table during the formal interview, though they were present. Finally, about 2 months after the process began, I was offered the position. When I tell this story to others I often hear, "I would not have gone through all of that." But I was glad I did. It meant they knew who I was and what they could expect, and sent the message that I would be working closely with a highly deliberative community. Deliberation takes time and effort, but judging by the quality of the staff at the school, and viewed in light of the mission of the school to teach the habits of mind necessary to be effective democratic citizens, the process was well worth the efforts.

This chapter describes in more detail how processes of shared decision making were put in place from the school's inception, and discusses the strengths and limitations of these approaches from the viewpoints of teachers, parents, and graduates. I begin by describing the challenges and benefits of staff governance. I then turn to parent participation, and end with ways in which students are involved in decision making at the school. Although this chapter will end with examples of how student voices are included in decision making at the school, the next chapter on curriculum will focus much more on that topic.

THE GOVERNANCE BOARD OF THE SCHOOL

Using its autonomy of governance as a pilot school, the staff created multiple layers of democratic governance structures in order to elicit inclusion and produce responsiveness for participants (Meier, 2000, 2002; Meier, Sizer, & Sizer, 2004). The governance structures include a governing board with the power to hire or fire the principal and set policies for the school, consisting of one-third teachers, one-third community members, and one-third parents, plus at least two student representatives. Any one of the constituencies on the board can veto any decision. A two-thirds vote in all three constituencies is required to pass any policy. Parent board members are elected by the Family Council, which consists of all parents. Teachers serve on a rotational basis. Teachers are responsible for making most policies for the school, such as hiring colleagues, developing curricula, planning special events, scheduling meetings, and more. The principal ostensibly works at the behest of the teachers and governing board. Further, any one teacher can veto any decision, as the decisions are made by consensus. This is possible, in part, since there are just 12 teachers and 2 administrators, whereas a larger staff would make such democratic structures much more difficult.

BROAD COMMUNITY AND FAMILY PARTICIPATION AT THE SCHOOL

In addition, there are many attempts, outside of these formal governing structures, to include parents and community members in decisions about the life of the school, some of which were described in Chapter 4. They include: the participation of community members, parents, teachers, and students participate in the 7th- and 8th-grade portfolio presentations; regular "family nights" are held for parents, teachers, students, and community members to eat and commune and to learn more about the curriculum or another theme; there are multiple school and community partnerships, internships, and community service opportunities for students; and a considerable amount of student voice is encouraged in the classroom (Knoester, 2010; Meier, 2000, 2002; Meier, Sizer, & Sizer, 2004).

I asked Meier, "Why is democratic decision making, or democratic staff governance, important to you?" This is how she replied:

> [There are] many reasons, but the very minimalist reason is that what I want teachers to be teaching kids is the habits of mind needed for democracy. It's hard to explore that if you're not exploring it for yourself. So, I want them to get engaged with me in exploring the question of democracy. What's it all about? Second of all, it's hard to convince kids that democracy is important if their teachers put up with not being treated in a democratic fashion. Thirdly, if teachers don't think they own the school, which, some teachers feel that way even if they're democratic decision makers . . . but, it helps. . . . It's hard to take responsibility for your colleagues' work. And finally, when I was a teacher, what I resented most was that I wasn't treated like an equal, in terms of important decisions about the school.

These words were echoed and confirmed in many of my interviews with Mission Hill School teachers. Kathy D'Andrea, for example, has been a teacher at Mission Hill School for more than a dozen years, working at various age levels. When asked what was most unique about working at Mission Hill School, this is how she responded:

> I think the most unique thing [about Mission Hill School], first of all, is that it's a staff-run school. And so, by giving teachers voice, you give them respect, you give them understanding that they have a responsibility, not just to the rest of the kids in this classroom, but all the kids in the school, the daily runnings of the school, interactions with all parents, not just their parents; you make teachers responsible for teaching other teachers, and then they realize they're capable of teaching other teachers, that they have a lot to offer.

It is clear from the above statements that democratic decision making is important, but not unproblematic. One key question that arises is: "Democratic for whom?" In other words, who is the "constituency" in the democracy? Despite the many governance structures put in place to include the voices of staff, parents, students, and "outside" community members, D'Andrea describes the school as a "staff-governed" school. Why is this considered democratic? Why is this democratic as opposed to, for example, one person having one vote? Meier pointed out in one of our interviews that if all parents and teachers had one vote, the parents would outnumber the teachers 10 to 1. So while the voice of parents is important, Meier and the founding staff of the school made the choice that the decisions about what happens in classrooms should be made by the people who are closest to the action: the teachers, and children, who are carrying it out.

STAFF GOVERNANCE AT MISSION HILL SCHOOL

It is first important to describe in more depth what is meant by *staff governance*. Given the above descriptions of shared governance that includes parents and other community members, the term *staff governance* may be misleading. However, it does touch on an important aspect of Mission Hill School governance—the fact that the staff makes many important decisions together. In most schools in Boston and elsewhere it is primarily the principal who makes decisions, large and small, relating to the school. In fairness, most schools also do not have the autonomies of pilot schools, so principals are under greater pressure to follow the mandates of the district office and teacher contracts.

Provided its autonomies as a pilot school, Mission Hill School teachers are charged with the responsibility of thinking through many decisions relating to curriculum, hiring, calendar, budget, and governance itself. This, of course, requires time. So part of the commitment teachers make in joining the staff is to spend an additional 5 hours per week meeting with colleagues. One of those hours is a "business meeting," with required attendance and shared decision making for all staff. Then there are various committee meetings and ongoing processes, such as a highly structured peer-review system. The remainder of the 5 hours is generally devoted to professional development meetings—in small groups called *houses,* in age pairs, or in the large group, and they generally focus on curricula, student assessment, and communication with parents. There are also three staff retreats per year, where key decisions about staffing, curriculum, budget, and other major issues are made, but this is also a time for staff to present curricular ideas for the next term and to receive critiques and feedback from colleagues. Staff members are paid an additional stipend beyond their union contract salary for this work, and the number and placement of hours dedicated to these tasks are well known in advance, and themselves a result of deliberation. They are almost never spontaneously planned, an important aspect in respecting the time of participants. D'Andrea summarized the experience well when she said this:

> You can't put one toe in the water, you gotta dive in until your head's covered. I don't mean you can't be on staff and say, "I can't take that on right now." But you're expected to be there. So what that means is . . . you are expected to be at meetings, you are expected to be communicating, to be available for meetings, to be there for all the kids, all of those things. And, as much work as it is, I can't imagine it any other way.

I asked one relatively new member of the staff, Melissa Tonachel, an experienced teacher in other public schools in the Boston area, to reflect on her first impressions of being part of a staff-governed school. She replied:

> Okay, so I think the disadvantage is time. And my spouse would say the same thing. And I really think that's it. It requires something else of us, logistically. The other things it requires of us are all positive: to be listening to different points of view, which again is what Reggio Emilia [an Italian town known for its progressive philosophy of education and a place Melissa had just visited] is all about (Wein, 2008), which is bringing in new perspectives all the time. I think that it engenders a really different and deeper sense of commitment to the school as a

body, and not just to "my kids" in "my classroom." As a new person, I don't have the personal relationships on which that's layered or that are layered on top of it. I'm in the process of developing those relationships . . . I so appreciate being able to know what's happening all around the school . . . I make a point of reading the newsletter . . . it gives me tremendous insight into what values people are placing and what kinds of activities . . . and it makes our practice public. That's another piece of it . . . if you're discussing everything together, your practice becomes public really quickly.

Another staff member, Amina Michel-Lord, reflected back to the 1st year that the school opened, and what struck her about the shared decision-making model of Mission Hill School. She was an assistant teacher at the time, and had been working for several years at another Boston public school, where the principal had the final word on almost all decisions, and it was hard to imagine a teacher standing up to the principal:

That reminds me of my first indication that Mission Hill was really different. It must have been my first year. We were having a house meeting in Emily Gasoi's room and we were supposed to be planning a family night on a specific day, which was approaching fast. And the staff was saying, "No, we're not ready for this. We're not prepared, it's coming too soon." But Debbie was saying, "No, but it's gone out in the newsletter, we said it was this day, that's what we said we were going to do, we need to stick to it." And I remember thinking, "Well, that discussion's over, we're having family night because that's what Deb said." And it was the teachers pushing back: Alicia, Emily, I don't remember who else was there, pushing back, holding strong to: "No, we just can't do it, it's not going to be right." And I remember sitting there going, "Wow, they're talking back to the principal. Ooooh. They're going to lose their jobs." And, you know, Deb loves a good argument, and they went back and forth. And it was decided, we weren't going to have the family night. And I was amazed! I was like, "Oh shoot, they really have a say-so." And Deb wasn't mad, she was just like, "All right. I still disagree, but we're going to go ahead and cancel it."

The Benefits and Challenges of Collaborative Decision Making

Among the challenges for teachers to share fully in the decision-making process at a school is the substantial amount of time that is required. Almost all of the teachers I interviewed spoke about the difficulty of giving time and energy to all of the responsibilities in their work and outside lives. For example, when asked about the disadvantages of shared decision making, one teacher replied:

> The time, as I'm sure you remember. The amount of hours that you put in is just a . . . it's a downfall, I think, because it impedes on you having a life outside of Mission Hill, but it's also an asset because it shows how dedicated people are to their jobs, that they will come in on a Saturday to get their work done, or they will stay until six o'clock in the night doing the different professional developments that we do, or they'll come at eight o'clock in the morning for those business meetings, and the house meetings, and then the age-pair meetings. Last week I had seven meetings in four days. So it ends up that you feel like you're lacking time to put into the things that you want in your classroom, but then it's also valuable because you think like a principal and the entire school is on your mind.

Staff Members Cannot be Passive in the Decision-Making Process

Another teacher gave an example of how the additional time given to discussion really does have an effect on how she has thought about particular issues:

> The fact that we can vote on most decisions is a really valuable asset of being at Mission Hill—that you know that your voice counts. So I remember the first time that I was sitting in one of those meetings and I was supposed to vote. I kind of sat there and I was like, "Well, I'm not going to put up my hand. So if I don't put up my hand is anybody going to notice?" Because I had an opinion, my opinion was very strong and it was against what the rest of the group was doing. It was about hiring a particular person. And I was sort of like, "Uh, no, I don't think that's a good idea." And because I didn't say anything I got found out. And they were like, "Uh, we noticed that you didn't vote. What's the deal?" And from that time on, I was like, "You know what? I guess my voice really does count."

Overfamiliarity Can Make Accountability Difficult

Even aside from the issue of time, there are clearly tensions and challenges to running a school in this way. One teacher described how the tendency to please one another, in order to make meetings go smoother, can sometimes get in the way of making difficult decisions, or to hold one another account-able. So attempts are made to counter this tendency:

> I remember Brian saying, "I'm going to push you on that. We just can't let that go," or, "I need you to take that next step," or, just, that it was okay . . . it's always been okay, and still is, to voice opposition. And it doesn't have to be nastily done, it can be done respectfully.

The Challenge of Changing Leadership

The principalship at Mission Hill School has changed over the years. Although Meier retains a position at the school as the director of new ven-tures she stepped down from the principalship in 2005, and her assistant and later co-principal, Brian Straughter, became the sole principal. However, in 2006, Straughter also stepped down, and a former teacher, Ayla Gavins, who had left Mission Hill School to become an administrator (academy leader) at nearby Orchard Gardens School, returned to Mission Hill School to become the new principal. The hiring processes were long and included the voices of every constituency of the school. One graduate of Mission Hill School, who at the time was an 8th grader and student representative on the governing board, said this about the process:

> Ayla was chosen by . . . you could say by Mission Hill. The search committee did a lot of the initial picking and choosing of people but the final decision was brought to the whole governance board. And when Ayla came to the board, there was this excitement she had about Mission Hill. She came to the final interview with this binder and she was like, "Here are my ideas." And she's like, "I don't even really know if all of them are going to come true." She's like, "But I have all these different ideas. And when I see programs I like, I just put them in this folder." And it was just totally a well-organized thing and everyone at Mission Hill was like, "Oh, I have so much faith in her." I think that's really why she was chosen.[1]

PARENT PARTICIPATION IN DECISION MAKING AT MISSION HILL SCHOOL

In terms of parents' role in decision making, there are many opportunities for participation, both formal and more informal. One teacher reflected on the importance of listening to parents and eliciting their insight, in this case about their own children:

A school has to be a place where families feel not only welcomed, but that they belong, that they are a significant presence, and a valued part of what we're trying to do with their children. [Otherwise], we're let out of some information about that child that only the parent has. So we, as teachers, can't ignore the knowledge of the family in seeing the child for more hours of the day than we do. Children suffer from not seeing the important adults in their lives working together to support them . . . but the other thing to say is that participation is going to look different, and presence is going to look different for everyone, and that's fine.

The Family Council at Mission Hill School

Another staff member characterized how the family council, a group that includes all Mission Hill School parents—even if only a small fraction of parents attend the regular meetings—has worked with the staff on recent issues:

We do have a family council, and over the past few years there has been more teacher/administrator involvement at certain sessions of the family council. The family council has come up with questions that are posed back to the staff and the administrator, for us to discuss and muddle through. So the family council and the staff have symbolically joined forces to discuss and iron out different issues within the school.

I asked parents if they thought that the family council was effectual, that if the family council was united and wanted something to happen in the school, that they could make that happen. Almost all of the parents said they thought that that was true. However, from the opening of the school, the family council (then called the *parent council*) was also fraught with struggles that caused a considerable amount of concern and tension in the school. One of those struggles, as was discussed in the previous chapter, was the question of whether those attending family council meetings seemed to represent the interests of the entire parent body, especially since those in attendance tended to be White. These concerns were raised in interviews I had with both parents and staff. One parent, for example, said the following:

I think early on at Mission Hill I felt like there was a lot, relatively speaking, for the size of the school. . . . there was a fair amount of parent representation. But I also know that there was not always an equal representation of all the kinds of families. You know, that it was much more of a White dominated group, and so that was something that there was a lot of conversation about. There was a lot of effort made to try to figure out how to shift that dynamic.

One parent explained why she was not able to go to the family council meetings:

> I don't think it's the principal that makes all the decisions, I think the parents make decisions because they have meetings, parent meetings, council meetings, parent council, although I don't go that much and the reason I didn't go is I'm a single mother. Also, I go to school myself, to learn this language. I don't get time to go there every time. But it looks like they let the parents of the school make decisions.

One teacher, who pointed to this as her greatest current concern about the school, described an effort she and others were making toward addressing this issue:

> Right now we have the family engagement committee, we've had that for a few years and we are trying some different things. . . . Wednesday night we're having a meeting for all parents of color to talk about their role in this school. What is it? What is it not? What would you like it to be? And they could say, "You know what? I really could care less." Or they could say, "Wow, I was just waiting for somebody to invite me."

Brian Straughter reflected on efforts he and others made to include a wider range of parents in the decision making, both at Mission Hill School and at his previous school, that point to how difficult the task of inclusion can be:

> I remember when I was at [my previous school]—and I know it's similar at Mission Hill—when we were trying to get more families of color out for some very important topics, one family said to me point blank, "There's no way that I could go to one of these meetings and talk as articulately as," and they named these families. And I'm not going to blame these families. And . . . I knew this family had things they would have loved to have shared that we could have learned from.

I asked Straughter to describe why or how the inclusion of more parents at council meetings might enrich the discussions and he gave this powerful example:

> [Most of the staff] hasn't experienced, many tragedies [in their lives]. I mean, we have kids coming to Mission Hill who know that someone last night got shot in the neighborhood. I never had to deal with that. And now I'm an adult and I still don't have to deal with it. Many families at Mission Hill, and in Boston, have experiences . . . I mean,

that are bad. And helping the staff to understand those experiences [is important]. We have to step into their shoes and understand more of where they're coming from.

Meier recognized that it may be impossible to bring all families, or even a close representation of all families, to all of the meetings, given the time constraints and other factors families must deal with. However, she insisted the issue of school "ownership" was crucial. Meier said the following about attempts to include all parents, and particularly parents of color, in the family council:

I didn't actually think that participation was as important, but what I thought was more critical was do they think of it as their school, whether they participate or not? So, there are a lot of good reasons for Black and Latino parents to be suspicious about whether the school belongs to them, about whether the teachers respect their children. And while I didn't always agree with everything [education scholar] Theresa Perry has said . . . the question she posed, "When people walk into the school, who do they think it belongs to?" is an important question. Everything we were doing was trying to address that question.

It was clear from my interviews that the Mission Hill School was able to create a space where parents generally felt welcome. One parent compared Mission Hill School to the schools her children now attend:

I think the parents were more connected at Mission Hill [compared with her children's new school] . . . that the teachers, the school community, the school administrative staff were more communicative. I do meet with their teachers but they are scheduled meetings. Issues with other children, if they arise, are handled very differently than they would have been at the Mission Hill School. . . . For the most part, not that it was perfect, but things would be addressed and talked about [at Mission Hill]. That doesn't happen in their new school.

Parents Feel Listened to by Teachers, Not Always by Others

One finding that became clearly identified in my interviews was that parents and teachers worked closely together in discussing particular children, and that parents noticed and appreciated that. In fact, 100% of the parents interviewed answered in the affirmative when I asked if they felt "listened to" by their children's teacher (although this was less true about the administration or the family council). For example, one parent, when asked about this topic, said the following:

I know that they [the teachers] always involve the parent as far as the children are concerned. They ask the parent what they think. I've always had them say to me, "Well [your son] did this so what do you think we should do? In house [suspension]? Do you think he should go home?" They've always called me . . . as far as that. And they always ask my input about his IEP [Individual Education Program] and what I think will work for him.

STUDENT INVOLVEMENT IN DECISION MAKING AT MISSION HILL SCHOOL

Students are also involved in the decision-making processes at Mission Hill School, from the youngest kindergarteners to the oldest 8th graders. In the next chapter, focusing on curriculum, I describe in much more detail how students make decisions affecting their own learning in the classroom. However, here it is important to note that there are also roles for students in making decisions affecting the whole school. For example, one graduate reflected on an occasion when she and her classmates were asked to participate in the decision of whether to hire a particular teacher:

I remember when I first realized the staff did run things. [It] was when I was in Alphonse's class [for 9 to 11 years old] and we had student teachers come in. I think we had three or four different student teachers come in, and I know Jenerra was one of them. And they all came in and they spent their time in the class, and then we had a class discussion about who we thought would fit in best at Mission Hill. That's the first time that we participated in making a decision that kind of changed the whole school.

As was mentioned previously, 8th-grade students serve official roles on the governing board of the school, with a vote on key decisions, including hiring and firing the principal. One graduate who had served on the governing board at Mission Hill indicated why it was important to include democratic processes in making important decisions, as opposed to allowing the principal to make all of the decisions:

Deborah Meier [could just make all of the decisions] . . . I mean, obviously, she's incredibly successful and known for her ideas and she's incredibly intelligent, but having everyone vote just kind of ensures that the decision is reflective of everyone's interests—like the best interests of the school—and it ensures that it's the best decision.

One parent reflected on the many ways she had seen shared decision making at the school, from students making decisions together in the classroom, to how she saw teachers working together at a recent staff retreat (most of which are also open to parents), and said the following:

> Well, since they take 3 weeks to decide a classroom name, that's the first thing that you hit as a citizen of the school. So that process is mindboggling to me and I don't know how anyone has the patience for it, but anyway. So, all the way from that up to the governing board, and . . . I've been to a couple of staff retreats, and I could see the collaboration that's involved. I don't feel like anybody is on their own doing their own thing. I feel like everybody knows everybody's business and decisions are made cooperatively. That's just the way it is.

CONCLUSION

While there are challenges and tensions within the decision-making processes at Mission Hill, there is an unmistakable ethos of shared decision making at the school. Some critics might argue that every person at the school should have one vote and that real democracy does not exist without that full inclusion. However, the founders and sustainers of the Mission Hill School decided to give the greatest amount of decision-making power to those adults who spend the most amount of time at the school and must implement whatever decisions are made, the teachers. Of course, that decision-making power could be taken away with a change to the negotiated contract between the Boston Teachers Union and the Boston Public Schools, and as Straughter described above, those forces do exist and at times overextend their power. For example, in the final months of writing this book, the school came under threat of being moved to a different location, against the wishes of the school community. Despite protests by the school community, district and city leaders, including the superintendent of BPS; the mayor and City Council have made plans to move the Mission Hill School to a location approximately 1.5 miles away from its current location and into a different school building and community. This move could prevent many of the current families from continuing to send their children to the school. So the fate of the school is not always in its own hands.

Still, with the autonomies granted to the school as a pilot school, the staff and governing board of the school have consistently attempted to distribute power broadly and kept the school small enough that the Faculty Council (full-time teachers) are able to reach consensus on important decisions affecting the school.

Barber (2003) wrote the following about democratic decision making:

> Reasonable choices are generally public choices. That is to say, they are choices informed by an extension of perspective and by the reformulation of private interests in the setting of potential public goals. To be reasonable is therefore not to deny Self, but to place Self in the context of Other and to inform it with a sense of its dependence on the civic polity. (p. 128)

In many schools parents are considered reasonable and even righteous when they appear at their child's school and advocate for his or her interest, even if it is at the expense of the interests of another child. Indeed, parents at Mission Hill are expected to attend family conferences and other meetings organized around the interests of their own children. However, with the institution of such bodies as a governing board, made up of one third parents, and the family council, and invitations to attend staff retreats and other meetings, it is clear that parents, along with the other constituencies of the school, are strongly encouraged to think about and participate in the decisions affecting the entire school, and not only those items that may relate directly to their own children. The tensions within the family council and in other bodies may be directly related to whether parents are thinking about private interests too narrowly.

Related to this, it is important to be aware of a growing body of research literature suggesting parents with cultural capital, and especially White and middle- and upper-class parents, mobilize their cultural capital to disproportionately affect decisions in schools (Horvat, Weininger & Lareau, 2003; Lareau & Horvat, 1999); and reason suggests the involvement of White parents at family council meetings at Mission Hill may be a manifestation of this pattern.

Although finding the right balance of parent representation on the family council is a struggle at the school, this struggle does not necessarily affect many of the important decisions that are made. Much of the actual decision-making responsibility is placed in the hands of the school's faculty—a decision made at the outset of the school, but a decision that is not without controversy. Nevertheless, the evidence from my interviews and my experience at the school suggests there exists a culture, and multiple avenues at Mission Hill, both formal and informal, in large and small groups, for public discussion and shared decision making around issues affecting the entire school, and especially among the faculty, who must take the lead on implementing the educational decisions they make together.

6

Overt and Hidden Curricula
at the Mission Hill School

The *sine qua non* of education is whether teachers know how to make complex subjects accessible to diverse learners and whether they can work in partnership with parents and other educators to support children's development.

–Linda Darling-Hammond, *The Right to Learn*, p. 294

A FRIDAY SHARE

Yesterday was another memorable Friday Share at Mission Hill. Friday Share is the weekly gathering of the whole student body at Mission Hill School to present to one another the week's work. It began in typical fashion. Students sat on the carpet in their designated classroom space, and a single row of chairs lined the walls for adults and middle school students.

Adults held up two fingers to indicate "Quiet, let's get started." After waiting for quiet, the MC, an 8th-grade student with a microphone in his hand, welcomed everyone and told the group what the opening song will be. He belts, "Good morning, Mission Hill!" And the students roared "Good morning!" in response. "The opening song for today is 'Rockin' Robin'" he called out, pointing to two large sheets of butcher paper with the lyrics clearly printed. Several teachers stood and joined the MC to lead the school in song, and the room filled with high-pitched voices belting the tune.

Next, representatives from each class from the West House (half of the school) took their turns to present—each class has the choice of either sending four students (no more), or the whole class together could perform a song or choral reading.

First, Geralyn's kindergarten/1st-grade class sent four students. Using a Q&A format, Geralyn asked the students what they had been working on this week. Three students held up bean seeds germinating in plastic bags. "What are you showing us?" Geralyn asked the first student into the microphone, then held the microphone near the first student's mouth. "We got the paper towel wet and put a bean inside," the first student responded. Geralyn moved to the next student. "What happened next?" "We put the bags in a dark place, in our cubbies, and these things started to come out," came the reply. "What is Cailyn pointing to, Jeremy?" Jeremy explained, "She's pointing to the root that is coming out of the bean." Next, Geralyn announced, "Now Aisha is going to read from her journal." Aisha looked down and read, "Today we went to check out bean seeds and mine cracked open. I could see a long stringy thing coming down." The three students with bean seeds held up the bags and walked around the front row of students and gave the students a closer look.

"Okay, thank you, Geralyn's class," the MC declared. "Next up is Kathy's class." Kathy, the 2nd- and 3rd-grade teacher in the West House, received the microphone from the MC and began to describe what the class was doing that week. "Like many of you, we have been taking care of monarch caterpillars this fall and something very exciting has been happening. Most of our caterpillars turned into chrysalises, and two of them emerged from them. We were able to capture the second one emerging on video. She then cued the video, on a large monitor in the corner of the room, and the students appeared highly engaged as they watched the insect break out of its transparent chrysalis and begin to pump its shivering wings.

Next it was our turn. It was hard to decide what to present this week. Several students wanted to share the giant paper mache bugs we made last week, others wanted to present the handmade books we were creating that included our research and photos of related art projects. But the choice of the majority was the original song we wrote together as a class, "The Buggy Blues." The song began several weeks ago, as a committee of students selected to write a draft as one of their options during project time. This group of four students brought their draft to the rest of the class during a morning meeting and several additions and edits were made. They asked if I could add some music to the piece. I put it to music using a simple blues progression, although the length of several lines had to be changed to fit with the music. Our class sings or plays music, often a drum or percussion circle, as a closing activity nearly every day, so we had been practicing the song for several weeks. We were ready. A student had the idea that the whole class bring sunglasses to school, which they did. But they waited until after the guitar introduction and just before the words began to slip them on— for added effect. The song was a hit. Students basked in the applause, and when we returned to the room students already began talking about the next song they wanted to write.

The rest of Friday Share was something of a blur, although I remember several middle schoolers presented carefully worded information about what they were learning in their media literacy class, and several students held up posters they had made in the form of a collage of cut-outs from magazine advertisements, and spoke about the racism and sexism they noticed in these ads.

The MC took back the microphone and introduced the final song: "Take Me Out to the Ballgame." It was a fitting selection, as the Red Sox were once again in the postseason, and excitement was in the air—judging by the number of Red Sox t-shirts worn by students. As the group sang the song for the second time, the principal pointed to a class and the students filed out of the library and back to class.

In this chapter I examine in detail the curriculum of the school, or Mission Hill School's response to the question, "What does education for democratic citizenship look like?" The mission statement of the school, presented in Chapter 2, describes the "habits of mind" that the founding staff of the school believed were central to effective democratic citizenship, and indeed, for many of the personal and professional pursuits the school hopes to prepare its graduates for.

The mission statement also makes special mention of the importance of the arts as a central form of communication in a democracy:

> Democracy requires citizens who are themselves artists and inventors—knowledgeable about the accomplishments, performances, products, and inventions of others but also capable of producing, performing, and inventing their own art. Without art we are all deprived.

The final section of the mission statement speaks to a belief about human nature; that people are social, and children are motivated to learn in large part out of love and caring for others, and the desire to share themselves and their work with others, to be part of a community that respects them.

In this chapter I describe in more detail the ways of thinking about human development and children's learning that lead to the goals articulated in the mission statement, and specific ways the curriculum is planned and carried out at various age levels, the rationale behind key decisions. This is followed by an evaluation of the curriculum based on how participants from various constituencies understand and reflect on their past experiences in relation to the Mission Hill School curriculum.

I begin with an overview of how Meier and other staff members understand Mission Hill to be part of a progressive education tradition, rooted in particular understandings about human nature, and how urban schools like Mission Hill can counteract social inequalities that often place students, and particularly working-class students and students of color, at a disadvantage.

PROGRESSIVE EDUCATION AND THE DEVELOPMENT OF HABITS OF MIND FOR CRITICAL THINKING

The educational approach of the Mission Hill School stands in stark contrast to the dominant culture of "covering" standards in chronological fashion and strictly limiting the movements and decision-making opportunities of students. The underlying principles guiding curricular decisions at Mission Hill are rooted in particular theories of human nature and learning in relation to what is necessary for students to become the kinds of people aspired to in the mission statement. In addition to these assumptions about human development, there is a set of critical social theories influential to staff at Mission Hill School about how racism, classism, sexism, and other forces of inequality impact schooling and must be taken into consideration when planning a curriculum that can live up to the ideals of the mission statement.

The central focus of the curriculum at the school is the development of five particular habits of mind, useful for effective democratic participation and deliberation, as well as in the academic disciplines. The five habits of mind listed below, articulated as questions, continually guide students when approaching a problem:

1. "What is the evidence?" (in other words, be skeptical),
2. "What is the relevance?" (or, why should I care?)
3. "How is this connected with other structures, forces, or facts?" (connections)
4. "From whose viewpoint am I looking?" (perspective) and
5. "How could it be different?" (conjecture).

The development of these habits of mind takes a long time, and at the Mission Hill School the habits are a central part of the curriculum starting in the youngest grades. In the older grades they are clearly and explicitly applied in the 7th- and 8th-grade portfolio papers, projects, and presentations. These habits of mind are written on posters in every classroom at the school and continually referenced throughout the grades; they even appear on the school t-shirts and other items where symbols of the school are represented, further indicating their centrality to the school's mission. The school believes it is important to articulate the long-term goals of education, not only the short-term tasks of learning discrete facts, skills, and concepts, even while these bits of knowledge also play a crucial role in curricula at the school.

Constructing Knowledge Takes Time

I asked Meier about the importance of allowing students to have decision-making capacities in school; this is how she replied:

It's the answer to the question that Dewey was asking. I want kids . . . to have the kind of mindsets and spirits that will enable them to take on the issues of democracy in the twenty-first century. So, I can't see, therefore, how a school which tells you always what to do . . . [can] prepare you for that. A school which doesn't honor disagreement and toughness of mind and skepticism can't do that. A school that doesn't challenge your capacity to have empathy for ideas, as well as people, that you might normally find offensive can't do that. I also know that people thrown into entirely new situations can't grow new ideas unless they grow them out of their old ideas. They can't have confidence in themselves if you told them everything they did before is wrong. So, on the other hand, it means learning is slow. You have to respect people's past experiences, and work with their expectations and experiences.

What is counter-hegemonic about this approach is that saying change is slow and can't happen overnight may seem to some observers that Meier does not value high curricular standards or appreciate the amount of knowledge it takes to be successful in a highly competitive market for college or high-paying jobs. This is the way, for example, some readers of Meier's blog on the *Education Week* website have interpreted her words (Meier, 2012). But the opposite interpretation is more accurate. Meier values curricular content greatly, and therefore believes that educators must be students of human nature and how children actually learn. Piaget's argument is counterintuitive; students form correct ideas out of their incorrect old ideas. But this is not an easy argument to make to skeptics who are impatient with students who do not learn "enough" and do so quickly; when memorizing information for a test, even though it is quickly forgotten, continues to satisfy a large number of educators and policymakers. This counterintuitive approach is reminiscent of Aesop's fable of the Tortoise and the Hare: Slow and steady wins the race. Meier attributes her ideas on these topics to the work of Jean Piaget and Eleanor Duckworth:

> [It requires] trust of kids and their own interests, passions . . . that curiosity [about children] was what I felt was fascinating about Piaget, influenced by Eleanor, and his stages, his way of respecting children, their world, not that [children] were wrong before . . . not that they were wrong, but imagine how did the world look to a child . . . in which they were exactly right?

Criticisms of Progressive Education in Urban Public Schools

Progressive education in the United States has come under a wide range of criticisms. For example, some critics point out that progressive, or "child-centered," approaches to education have been generally associated with private schools, schools that serve mostly White middle- and upper-class students, suggesting such an approach is inappropriate for urban working-class students or students of color (Bernstein, 1977; Delpit, 1995). This critique was raised repeatedly in interviews with staff at Mission Hill, indicating awareness among staff of these controversies. Despite these assumptions, however, it is well known by Mission Hill staff that Meier, among other progressive educators, is recognized for founding successful progressive schools in working-class African American and Latino/a neighborhoods in New York and Boston (Bensman, 1987, 1994, 1995, 2000). I asked Meier if she thought progressive education appears differently when conducted in urban working-class neighborhoods, as opposed to schools for economically or socially elite populations:

> Because [teachers] start off with the assumption that upper-class kids are smart, or because their responses to us are more like ours and therefore we acknowledge, we recognize them as smart, [progressive education is] a little easier [in more upper-class settings].
>
> Because their answers to the questions are the same ones we would answer. So, we're less often jarred into thinking, "Is this kid stupid?" since the kids are more likely to know the answers we'd want them to give, or the way of being polite, or the way of showing respect. When those ways are more different it takes more out of us to try to make sense of it. But what you're trying to create is not that different. And you can't learn how to respect your ideas more in an environment where people are calling you stupid, where they're labeling you, I don't care what the culture is, I would say, that would be true.

Progressive education in urban public schools is difficult to do well. However, the work of Meier and others has proven that it is possible, and well worth the effort.

FOSTERING POSITIVE IDENTITY DEVELOPMENT WITH STUDENTS

One way that Mission Hill School staff is mindful of how class, race, and gender inequalities have negatively impacted schooling in the United States, and must be counteracted, is by paying close attention to the identity development of students. Studies show that many working-class students and boys and girls of color come to harmful conclusions about themselves during the schooling process, such as thinking "I am not smart," or that "School is not for people like me" (Dance, 2002; Grant & Gomez, 2001;

Knoester, 2009; Noguera, 2003, 2009). Mission Hill staff have theorized that these messages, which some scholars call the result of the "hidden curriculum" in schools (Apple, 1995), can be sent to students in a variety of ways, as was briefly discussed in Chapter 4. They may include staffing schools with teachers from dominant races and cultural groups rather than with people who reflect the school's demographics, treating parents with suspicion and disrespect when they enter the school building, tracking students in "high ability" and "low ability" groups, creating competition wherein some students are "winners" and others "losers," using culturally insensitive or exclusive curricula, spending a large amount of time and energy keeping students quiet and "orderly," and using teaching techniques and materials that are oppressively boring and barely relevant to the current lived experiences of students.

Developing Curricula Sensitive to the Identity Development of Students

Mission Hill School staff has instead instituted a variety of approaches and practices that keep the identity development of students at the forefront. The rationale is that a student's identity is a much more powerful and long-lasting motivational force than the accomplishment of learning any particular set of facts or concepts in a short amount of time that may be quickly forgotten, all while reinforcing hierarchies among students. While cramming short-term content knowledge in the classroom may appear to some, perhaps especially those most concerned with test scores, as a productive learning environment, students who fail to succeed in this type of enviroment are likely to develop identities that include seeing themselves as "not smart," which can negatively affect their long-term motivation to learn in school.

One basic principle of the approaches practiced at the Mission Hill School is a rejection of the idea that students need competition or harsh punishments to be motivated to learn. Rather, students are motivated by the desire to be part of a welcoming and accepting community with other people they respect and who respect them, and by the confidence that is gained from being given the opportunity to solve difficult problems and create beautiful and meaningful work, and being noticed and respected for doing so.

Sending Positive Messages Through the Hidden Curriculum

Following are a few examples of how these principles are carried out at the school. Some of these overlap with what I described in Chapter 4, but here with a greater focus on what might be considered the hidden curriculum:

1. All classes are multi-aged and there is no tracking or long-term ability grouping, so students are almost always working and learning among a heterogeneous group of peers. And mixed-aged pairs, such as a student from a 4th/5th grade class and another from a K/1 class can frequently be seen working together at various times. Students who qualify for special education services largely receive services within their primary classroom.

2. Every Friday the entire school gathers in the library for Friday Share. These half-hour meetings begin and end with whole-group singing, but the bulk of the meetings consists of members of half of the classrooms per week sharing a piece of what they have been working on in class. Teachers often rehearse the presentations with the students, so even the youngest students practice publicly speaking about their work (and their identities as students) in front of a large audience. Every student in the school speaks to the rest of the school at least once a year, often several more times. This is a powerful way for students to make public their identities as interesting and engaged students and creative problem solvers.

3. The walls and hallways of the school are galleries of student artwork and classroom projects, and several drafts are made of most projects, in order to make work of all students presentable, interesting, and worthy of positive feedback.

4. Most curricular themes (a topic I will turn to in the next section) culminate with a performance or presentation of some kind, often for the parents of students in the classroom, but also for peers throughout the school. These culminating projects in each theme are generally beautiful products, such as a drawing, a beautifully bound book, or a speech or play, that are the result of multiple drafts or rehearsals and worthy of praise from those who view the result (Berger, 2003; Knoester, 2008).

5. The classrooms are generally organized to be informal, homelike spaces, often with comfortable chairs or couches, lamps, plants, and pets; and most teachers are called by their first names.

6. At the end of the 5th grade students review their archive of collected work from previous years and write an autobiography of themselves as students, which they publish in a book with similar essays from other 5th-graders, along with a self-portrait of each. These books and an oral reading of their essays are presented at a celebration breakfast for parents, peers, and staff.

7. Students graduate from the Mission Hill School only after completing and defending intense portfolios of work that show their competence in each subject area, but which involve a large amount of personal choice on the part of students. This is another topic to which I will turn later in this chapter.

Each of these practices provide powerful opportunities for students, making it more difficult for Mission Hill School students to conclude about themselves that they are "not smart," or that school is "not for someone like me." Students take a great amount of ownership in their own learning, and their work and ideas are regularly made public and often celebrated, if only after first being critiqued in a safe, noncompetitive classroom environment.

Not all of these educational approaches are carried out without controversy. Later in this chapter I include a section on critiques that are given by parents, staff, and students to some of these approaches. Most of the critiques have to do with a perceived lack of rigor, since the school has made the conscious choice of allowing opportunities for curriculum to emerge from children, as opposed to the more traditional approach in which teachers "cover" a wide range of topics in a short amount of time in a top-down fashion and blame students if they cannot remember these topics or make use of them during testing season.

Building Citizenship and Community with Behavioral Expectations

One aspect of the critique that progressive education is not suitable for working-class students or students of color relates to how behavior expectations are communicated. Since the Primary Discourse (Gee, 1996), or cultural assumptions and ways of communicating of White, middle-class students is similar to the Discourse valued in schools, these White, middle-class students may not require the "structure" of behavioral expectations made explicit and enforced with rigid top-down management (Bernstein, 1977; Bourdieu, 1984). To some observers of Mission Hill School, the appearance of classroom settings and curricula that are somewhat informal indicates that the behavioral and academic expectations are not clear enough for the working-class students or children of color in the school, leading to miscommunication and perhaps unfair consequences. In fact, this possibility is often most on the minds of Mission Hill teachers because there is an element of truth to this critique: The discourses and dispositions valued in schools, including those at Mission Hill, often do favor the Primary Discourses of certain cultural groups as opposed to others (Gee, 1996). But while students at Mission Hill call teachers by their first names, for example, and there are comfortable places to sit in the classroom, there is still a strong belief at the school that the behavioral and academic expectations must be made as explicit as possible, and these practices can perhaps send mixed messages to students—calling teachers by their first names might be a form of disrespect, for example.

Making expectations clear is accomplished using a variety of class and school meetings, one-on-one discussions, written assignments and posters, skits in the classroom and at Friday Share, and other practices. For example, there are two clear school rules at Mission Hill School: Work Hard and Be Kind (also known to the community as the Mission Hill Way). These two rules, along with the habits of mind, are prominently posted in every class-room in the school. At the beginning of the school year communicating these rules is given top priority. In the hallway outside of the office a wall is dedicated to these two rules. On one side are dozens of photographs of students "working hard," and on the other side there are notecards on which are written specific examples of students "being kind."

At one point the school staff decided to use a set of books published by the Northeast Foundation for Children (Charney, 2002) to help with the important and ongoing curriculum of creating a school culture that values kindness and hard work, and makes these values explicit. So these values are communicated in a variety of ways, although there can also be more done to improve these goals. Specific individual cases at times require heavier interventions, and even unique educational arrangements beyond anything described in the literature noted above.[1] I will return to these topics in the last section of this chapter.

EDUCATION FOR DEMOCRATIC CITIZENSHIP

Disciplinary Content Presented Within Thematic Units

The overt curriculum, or openly stated curriculum, at Mission Hill School is framed under an umbrella of three sequential whole school interdisciplinary themes each year. The purpose of this approach is for students to learn and teach one another across grade levels, at the Friday Share, for example, and so the school can share resources, such as books, guest speakers, attend work-shops together, and generally share ideas, allowing more in-depth learning to take place. Further, since the thematic units are offered on a 4-year rotational basis, students experience learning within these themes twice during their time at Mission Hill, building on what they learned 4 years previous. Each year the themes are science, U.S. history/social studies, and an interdisciplin-ary investigation of an ancient civilization. The themes are broad enough that within each teachers are able to create unique smaller themes, activities, projects, and inquiries within their classrooms. According to Meier:

> The idea of a whole school theme I did suggest, it came out of my
> experiences at the [Central Park East] Secondary School. It worked
> at the Secondary School, [so I thought] maybe it could happen in the
> elementary school, because at Central Park East [elementary school]
> there wasn't much collaboration around subject matter, but some

collaboration around pedagogy. So I thought if we all were studying the same thing maybe that would bring a sort of unity to the [Mission Hill] school. And I also know that I was concerned with the question, "Is it possible for kids to explore issues of race?" We needed a school where we could talk about race.

Although the exact themes have varied over the years, the U.S. History/social studies themes were generally the following, on an annual rotating basis: U.S. History Through the Eyes of African Americans, The Peopling of America, The World of Work, and Government and Elections (or more generally, Who Counts?). These themes alternated from fall to spring (the "Who Counts?" theme was always planned to coincide with an autumn national election season). Each of these social studies themes are also called The Struggle for Justice, as they all included as central components issues of inequality in the United States and how various groups in U.S. history have fought against those inequalities. The winter theme (January through March) has generally been one of four ancient civilizations: Maya, Greece, China, and Egypt. The third theme (alternating between fall and spring each year) was around either natural or physical science. For many years the natural science theme included a schoolwide study of the life cycle of monarch butterflies. Each class either found or ordered dozens of monarch caterpillars, and students carefully observed their development over time and conducted research projects along with their direct observations, followed by a study of, for example, the life cycles of other insects, or schoolyard ecology.

There is some danger with choosing particular themes, since this might send the message that other themes are not worthy of study. That was certainly not the intention. But the curriculum cannot be all things to all people, especially when the school decided to take on a small number of themes in depth, rather than covering all important topics. Choices had to be made, but these themes were also not entirely arbitrary. Themes were chosen because they were thought to have some immediate interest for children, allowed students to see real-world connections between what they learned about in school and their outside lives, and allowed students to better understand their context in the world. They were also chosen because they are broad and interesting enough to allow for rich explorations within them that allow students to practice the habits of mind of critical thinking. Still, controversies arise at times when parents, students, or staff suggest that a different ancient or modern civilization be studied, or that particular areas are never studied in depth. Further, there are ongoing discussions among the staff about how various skills and knowledge are developed as students matriculate. What literacy skills are being developed in which grade, for example? How can the school provide ample opportunities for students to develop increasingly sophisticated sets of knowledge, skills, and dispositions?

Teachers Design Curriculum Within Broad Schoolwide Themes

How the themes are studied in individual classrooms has varied, depending on the teacher and the age level. Also, the one add-on to the thematic units across the grade levels is a separate hour-long focus on math, since it was decided several years ago that not enough attention was paid to math within the themes. The school eventually adopted a specific published curriculum for the elementary grades, *Investigations* developed by TERC, and another curriculum for the middle school grades, *Connected Mathematics Program*, both of which were adopted by the entire Boston Public School system.

The schoolwide themes listed above are chosen to be large umbrella-like themes, within which teachers plan many individual and individualized lessons and projects. The benefit of planning smaller lessons within larger themes is that students are more likely to see connections between what they learn one day and the next, and they can feel a sense of immersion, since the entire school is often decorated with theme-related information and artwork. The result is a momentum and mutual enthusiasm that can build around theme-related ideas within the school's student culture. Individual classes often put on various performances and invite other classrooms to see, and this creates opportunities for students to learn from one another.

In the following sections, teachers at each grade level provide specific examples of lessons or projects they have taught within the themes. Teachers often follow their own passions and interests while planning lessons within a theme. This is encouraged at Mission Hill School because a deep understanding of content knowledge is necessary to help students connect to what may interest them within an area, and allows a teacher to help students see connections from one content area to the next. Further, if teachers are passionate about a topic, they are more likely to continue learning about it outside of school, which is helpful to gain the deep knowledge necessary to make the subject accessible to students.

CURRICULUM IN AN EARLY CHILDHOOD CLASSROOM

In the early childhood classrooms, the curriculum largely emerges from the child—with many opportunities for imaginary play, including the use of drawings and journaling, and through the use of learning materials that allow children to discover patterns and forces of nature in the world. There are frequent sing-alongs, class discussions, and individual or whole-group inquiries, as well as teacher-directed assignments that give students opportunities to make decisions and solve problems. Early childhood teachers also use the schoolwide themes to frame various inquiries with their students. Because many of the themes are quite abstract, such as an ancient civilization, early childhood teachers often begin themes with topics that are more familiar to children.

As in all classrooms at Mission Hill School, early in the year early childhood teachers focus on building a respectful classroom community. For example, at the beginning of each year early childhood teacher Jada Brown and her class create a class constitution—rules to abide by in the classroom—that allows students to feel ownership and loyalty to the rules they created and give students an early chance to practice democratic skills such as negotiating with others to create a common document:

> In the beginning of the year we talk about what the rules are in the classroom, and it's not a set of rules that I end up making, it's a set of rules that the kids come together and they say, "These are the things that we need to be safe and happy in our classroom." And so they work together, with of course me there, and [assistant teacher] Joanne there, but it's a document that they sort of put together themselves, and they hold each other to it.

Kathy D'Andrea described how she thinks about the thematic units in her early childhood classroom. In this case, she describes how, during the whole-school theme of "Who Counts?" (about government and elections), she drew on environmental leaders to inspire her students to learn about struggles for a cleaner and healthier planet within a social studies theme:

> It's interesting because even though we have these [themes], we're allowed to do emergent curricula within them [following the interests of children]. So, for example, this fall, we're studying voice, or "who counts?" However, you have to think about what that's going to look like for 5-, 6-, and 7-year-olds. And so, one of the people that I first chose to share with them about using her voice was Wangari Mathai, from Kenya. She used her voice to plant trees, trees of peace. I could have chosen anybody who used their voice. But I chose an environmentalist, a woman, the first person to get their doctoral degree at the University of Nairobi. So, those were all messages that I wanted to send. They learned about other people too, and they actually ran with the environmental education piece, they said that's what they wanted to do. So those are places where I would not have been able to do that, I wouldn't have been able to allow them to use their voice if I was completely worried about MCAS, [Massachusetts standardized

test] instead of [asking], "where's the depth of knowledge? Where's the democratic society in this classroom? Where is their molding of their [own] learning?"

Early childhood teacher Melissa Tonachel, one of the newer teachers hired at Mission Hill School, recently visited the Italian town of Reggio Emilia, well known for its philosophy of early childhood education, and very much respected by teachers at Mission Hill. Tonachel indicated how her teaching at Mission Hill was similar in important ways with that of Reggio Emilia:

> I think that the focus on democracy is primary, among the similarities. The effort to have children act as . . . so talking about Reggio Emilia, the vocabulary changes because they have such a clear [and distinct] vocabulary, but they talk about children as protagonists . . . not beings that need to learn things, or that have deficits, such as, "They can't walk yet." They don't talk about children in that way, they talk about what they *can* do, what they bring to the learning process. And the teachers regard themselves as researchers, every day in the classroom. So they're always learning about how children learn in order to inform the next thing they do. They have long projects that span months, and so there are these similarities [to Mission Hill] just in how we think about learning.

D'Andrea used an example from mathematics to illustrate how she strategized about meeting the needs of a wide range of learners in her classroom and assessed students based on their work:

> What I have to do is put together a variety of different activities that are accessible, so, for example, the Vermont Exemplars [a type of math problem]. I love the Vermont Exemplars, because you can access them as a kindergartener, as a 1st-grader, and you can access them as a 2nd-grader. So . . . my 1st-graders who were working on a 2nd-grade level can . . . come out with 2nd-grade explanations and thinking, and my kindergarteners can draw pictures and do math drawings. So an example of one would be a written math problem with big font and a big space to write. One would be, "The kindergarteners like to make snowmen. They made three snowmen. Their teacher gave them buttons for eyes and nose. How many buttons did they get?" So they have to figure out, one, how many snowmen? Then they have to figure out how many eyes and a nose, and not make buttons all down the chest, and make buttons for the mouth, and think about what 3+3+3 is. And some kids write "3x3=9." Some kids write "3+3+3." Some kids draw the snowmen and count them

and say, "Nine." Some kids draw the three snowmen and give me no answer. Some kids draw seventeen snowmen. And you get to have a view into the child's understanding of what their thinking is.

Culturally Relevant Pedagogy

It can be hard to study an ancient civilization with young children because the idea of "long ago and far away" is highly abstract, and there are more immediate aspects of life that are still confusing and inherently interesting to children. So Jada Brown begins each year's ancient civilization theme with a study and celebration of each of her student's skin tones, families, and cultures, beginning with a life-sized self-portrait, which she hangs prominently on the walls of the classroom. She explained that the importance of studying diverse cultures in the classroom is to "normalize" each student's culture, and to send the message to all students that "School is a place for people like me":

> They paint themselves, they do their hair, they do their faces, outfits that they want, so it shows their personality as well, and you can actually see the difference between the two years the kids are in my room. So in kindergarten we have one child who stuck three or four buttons on himself, and we put it up. But then the next year he had a full outfit, so you see the progression of thinking about yourself, and how you want to put yourself together and represent yourself. And Jeanne [the art teacher] does a lot with the self-portraits too. . . . Then they bring in different foods [they like]. We've had families bring in Somali food, we've had different teas, scones, we've had treats from Colombia, we've had music from Ethiopia—we learned the Escapa. It's to set the stage so it's not, "Ewww, what's that? Uggghhh. Why are they wearing stuff like that?" There have been people who have come in, and I had one family come from Senegal, and he came in his complete Senegalese garb, put his daughter in her Senegalese garb, and did the national anthem of Senegal, and he cried. He cried.

Although this is just a small sample of how early childhood teachers at Mission Hill School think about and plan curricula for their classrooms, in relation to the whole-school thematic units and building a democratic culture in their classrooms, it is possible to see here how teachers allow students to bring much of themselves into the curriculum, allowing students to learn from one another and develop a respect for one another's cultural assumptions at a developmentally appropriate level. Students also are decision makers who learn how to deliberate on classwide agreements such as a set of rules, and who are given opportunities to solve math problems by devising multiple strategies that make sense to them, and who are given a lot of time to play with ideas as well (McLaughlin, 2012; Meier, Engel, & Taylor, 2010).

CURRICULUM AT THE MIDDLE CHILDHOOD LEVEL

In the middle childhood classes, ages 7 to 11, students are immersed in the thematic units chosen by the school and creatively planned and designed by each teacher for his or her specific classes. In these grades, students are more capable of thinking and speaking with abstract terms and concepts. Imagining an ancient civilization is still a stretch, for example, but students become fascinated and immersed in these themes, allowing deeper understanding than would be possible in a shorter 1- or 2-week unit, as is typical in most schools. I asked three middle childhood teachers to describe their favorite curricular themes and units they have planned and taught.

Alphonse Litz described the following unit he taught within the whole-school natural science theme. He explained how one of his favorite units was the study of the human body within the whole-school theme:

> I remember the one I used to love to do for natural science was the human body. Kids loved it because [they] feel really smart learning the names of the bones or diseases while they create skeletons and drawings of muscular systems. People from [Boston University] Medical Center came in and we were dissecting chicken legs and looking at muscles and there were so many entry points [for students to become interested], but it took me forever [to plan]. For every hour I had the kids I spent two or three hours planning. And I had taught this for years, you know, thinking of readings that connected to it, but I could teach the whole range of learners when I was really well provisioned and had [appropriately leveled] readings for them, and could thread their interests. There were fun projects . . . one that came to mind and connected the dots so well for kids was studying hinge joints, pivot joints. What kids did was make joints at the wood working table and they were built to scale and they worked. They had hinge joints for the elbows and knees and tennis balls and PVC pipes for ball joints and they had different bands that represented tendons and the muscles could contract and expand and they were just beautiful. Physicians came in from BU and said, "Wow, these are so beautiful, we could use these as models for teaching." And the students' writing was rich—such as the interviews [they conducted with health professionals], and the thank-you notes they wrote to all the people that came in—and this went on for months.

James McGovern, another 4th- and 5th-grade teacher, described a unit he taught during the World of Work whole-school theme, in which he led his class through an exploration on business and ethics:

> We designed t-shirts to sell for charity, as part of our World of Work unit, and we had chosen an orphanage in Guatemala to raise money for. But, as part of our study, we learned about sweatshops, and about worker rights, and about the economics of small business, and we did not want to buy cheap t-shirts from Wal-Mart, since we didn't feel comfortable about where they were made. So we found a place that made fair-trade t-shirts with organic cotton in the United States. It took a little research, because most of the companies that we looked into at first were in England and other places overseas, and they charged a fortune for the shirts. But we eventually did find a way to do it inexpensively enough to sell the shirts and make enough of a profit to send money to the orphanage.

McGovern described an ethical challenge faced by the class with immediate relevance to the school community:

> While doing that, the students had to go through all kinds of challenges to learn how to produce this product. They designed the t-shirts, the images, the slogans—three different ones—they chose the colors of the shirts, chose the fact that they were going to make shirts, instead of greeting cards, or bags. They did marketing surveys, they came up with a name for our not-for-profit corporation, and we had to get the capital. Toward the end of this, Mission Hill School t-shirts also became available. They were designed by an 8th-grader, and they were going to be for sale. And it became known to us that they were considering using a not-fair-trade manufacturer. And my class was outraged. They said, "We've spent so much time learning about this, how can our school give money to a business that is paying people in China or Pakistan or India, 35 cents a week to make these shirts?" So they wrote letters to the office, to "Whom It May Concern," because they didn't know who was responsible for this decision. And they wrote about sweatshops, and they wrote about workers' rights, and they wrote about the ethics of the decisions that we make and how we spend our money. I had to remind them that we are one community, and that accusations and confrontational language won't often get what you want when you're trying to persuade someone. So there were many rewrites.
>
> They changed their mind, the school, when they found out that we were doing this and people said, "Wait a minute, we can find a way

to do this inexpensively. They did, why can't we?" So it turned out the letters became unnecessary. But sometimes in the political process, just the fact that you're willing to take a stand, even though you haven't fought the fight yet, is enough to affect change.

Jenerra Williams, a 2nd- and 3rd-grade teacher, described her favorite unit as one she planned for the whole-school theme of United States History Through the Eyes of African Americans:

> I've taught this one twice, and both times I thought it was my best [thematic unit]—the Struggle for Justice—the African American experience. The reason that it's always been my best is because I'm the most connected to it. Not just because I'm a Black woman, but because I'm passionate about those issues and what happened in the 1950s and 1960s and how they affect what's happening now, not just with me, but with the kids that I teach. The first time that I taught it we looked at it with an art lens. And we used artists' paintings, poems, and songs to pull out the issues of the time. And the kids analyzed art, and created art, that spoke to all of those issues in the Civil Rights Movement. And the second time, which is the one that I really thought was the best, we looked at that theme through black and white photographs. And every new idea, issue, question that I wanted to present to them we learned about it through a photograph. They learned how to pick a photograph apart and get out what they needed from it. And we took black and white photographs. We recreated and restaged the Walgreens sit-in counter, or Little Rock Nine students going to school, whatever it was, having to put yourself in that place.

These examples demonstrate that in a school where teachers and students are able to conduct meaningful in-depth explorations of complex topics, rather than quickly glossing over many unrelated facts in order to prepare for a test, that quality student work and meaningful connections can take place. These teachers described how they drew on multiple intelligences, rich collaborations across various groups, students' inherent interest in issues of inequality and social justice, and multiple drafts and rehearsals to create culminating presentations that were worth positive recognition and that ultimately built the confidence, skills, and positive academic identities of students.

These were certainly the elements that guided my thinking as I planned and led units of study as a teacher of 9- to 11-year-olds. For example, during one spring unit, while the entire school was studying physical science I decided (after extensive consultation with colleagues) to focus with my class on astronomy. We were just coming off an exploration of ancient Greece, wherein students had created beautifully bound books of original creation myths that featured various Greek gods and goddesses. We had held a symposium with Greek food and music, and partook in a philosophical debate on the meaning of the word *courage,* in which students stood up and made speeches about the courage they saw in their classmates. After deep immersion in meaningful explorations such as this it is sometimes difficult to make a transition to an entirely new topic.

So I decided to begin our spring physical science unit by pointing out and inquiring into remnants of ancient Greece in our current lives, focusing on the names of the days of the week and months of the year, and planets in our solar system, many of which were named after Greek gods. I encouraged students to practice the habit of mind of *connection*s (asking "How is what I am learning connected to what I already know?") to notice how our daily use of these words were connected to ancient beliefs, and the habit of *relevance* (asking "Why does it matter?") by asking what they knew about how days of the week and months of the year were determined and what this might have to do with the movements of our planet. I read aloud stories to the students about ancient astronomers such as Pythagoros, Hipparchus, and Aristotle. As a group, we tried to understand how these men understood the composition of the universe and various bodies' movements, and how these understandings compare to current understandings. Then, drawing on the habit of mind of *evidence* (asking "How do you know what you know?") I challenged students to explain why some theories of our planet and the solar system could be more correct than others. And if ancient astronomers were known as brilliant, how is it that their theories could be so different from current understandings? This, of course, drew on the habit of mind of *perspective* (asking "From whose perspective am I looking?"), and the contrasting knowledge and experiences people in ancient times might have access to as compared with modern times. These discussions also drew on the habit of mind of *conjecture* (asking "How could things have been different?"), requiring students to imagine a different world, and also how things could have been different had particular discoveries not been made.

These discussions continued throughout the unit, as I read aloud many books and articles focusing on these topics, and students chose books and articles of their own to read. We observed the movements of the moon through a telescope in the classroom and outdoors. I organized a family trip to the telescopes at Boston University one evening, where we saw the rings around Saturn, the spot on Jupiter, and moons around both of these planets. The whole class also had the opportunity to visit the infrared telescope control center at the Harvard-Smithsonian astrophysics lab in Cambridge. We had a guest speaker come in, who was the former director of the Harvard-Smithsonian astrophysics lab, and students took detailed notes in their journals about their observations of the moon and had debates about where they predicted they would see it next, and in what phase (again, drawing on the habit of mind of *evidence*).

The culmination of the unit was a long-term project that involved each student in the class choosing a famous astronomer about whom they would become an expert. Some students chose ancient astronomers, like those listed above, and others chose more recent astronomers or physicists, such as Copernicus, Galileo, and most recent of all, Stephen Hawking. Each student chose a different theorist. Their task was to understand their scientist or astronomer's view of the universe, to summarize it in a two-page paper (several drafts of which were written to correct for grammar, style, and conventions), and to make a model of the solar system according to his or her theories. Students were then asked to create an aesthetically appealing poster board with information and pictures about their astronomer placed next to their model of the solar system (models were constructed from a range of materials, including Styrofoam balls, bent wire, paint, different colored clay, all provided by the school, so as to avoid disadvantaging students without these materials at home).

The finale of the study involved arranging the displays in chronological order around the classroom and inviting in other classrooms from around the school, as well as students' parents or guardians, to see our space museum. On the days the museum was open the presenting students dressed in black and brought in flashlights. We turned off the classroom lights, darkened the windows, and played eerie "space" music as background. As museum guests entered the classroom, they made their way around the museum of historical astronomers, and the presenting students explained their work to visitors using their flashlights to help focus attention.

Students heard well-deserved compliments about their work from nearly every visitor who came. Adults asked challenging questions, and the presenting students almost always rose to the occasion, further impressing their audience. In addition, this museum allowed the rest of the students in the school to enhance their understanding of physical science and astronomy through our research and presentations.

A significant number of learning goals were reached by the end of this unit. As indicated above, the habits of mind for critical thinking were practiced throughout. When inquiring into the etymology of words, the historical record of scientific discovery, debating the merits of contrasting astronomical theories, and imagining where they might see the moon next, students put the habits of mind to work. Then, the museum set students up for authentic compliments on their work by adults and peers alike, which allowed students to strengthen their identity development as serious and engaged students. Detailed note taking and writing was involved with various aspects of this thematic unit, reading for information, and a significant amount of mathematical reasoning was involved when discussing the size and distance of various celestial bodies, building models, and learning about how astronomy could be used for ship navigation using the Pythagorean theorem, among other tasks.

Although science units do not often focus on issues of social justice, as compared with social studies units, within this unit we were able to discuss issues surrounding the persecution of Galileo and other scientists who dared question religious orthodoxy, as well as issues of gender discrimination, such as the fact that educational opportunities were often not available to girls, but that there were nevertheless outstanding women astronomers in history, such as the 4th-century Egyptian scholar Hypatia. Similarly, racial discrimination prevented many men and women of African descent from accessing education, and yet, outstanding Black astronomers such as Benjamin Banneker have made significant discoveries and contributions. Both Hypatia and Banneker were chosen by students for in-depth study and presentation in our museum.

MIDDLE SCHOOL/ADOLESCENT CURRICULUM

The middle school at Mission Hill School consists of 6th-, 7th-, and 8th-grade students taking classes in the areas of math, science, humanities, art, media literacy, and physical and health/sex education. Middle school students also take part in an internship called School/Community Internship (SCI) as well as have the opportunity to join a variety of before- and after-school sports and activities. However, in 7th and 8th grade the bulk of the work done by students is in preparation for the portfolios they must create and defend in front of a panel of teachers, their parents, an outside community member, and a younger peer. Students must pass each of their portfolios in order to graduate from the school. In this section, I focus largely on two unique aspects of the middle school program at Mission Hill School: the course on media literacy and the portfolio process.

The following discussion took place among two sisters, their mother, and myself. The sisters are graduates of the school and are now both in college. Several interesting and relevant topics were raised in our discussion, particularly on the impact of their course on media literacy—which the sisters believe helped them to see television and magazines through a more critical lens—and a variety of ways in which the middle schoolers were both part of the entire school community and slightly removed from it:

> Graduate 1: I liked that in 8th grade, you were separate from the rest of the school. You were learning about media literacy, you were learning about the Holocaust. And everybody else wasn't learning

about those issues just yet. Because those are issues for older kids to understand that younger kids might not be able to comprehend right now. So those were really good things to open our eyes.

Graduate 2: It definitely ties into [the school's focus on] social justice and the way that they want us to think about ourselves . . . to be ourselves and to view the things that we see and the people that we talk to.

Mother: It was a developmental thing. In 2nd grade they're not going to know what slavery is. They don't know what it means. But I just think that everything was deliberate in how the curriculum was set up—well thought out—it wasn't just thrown together.

Graduate 1: And we wouldn't go to Friday Share and talk about a bunch of people dying. We would go there and try to find things that the younger kids could connect with too, that we could show what we learned. So it wasn't like the younger kids were being exposed to things that they shouldn't be exposed to. It was definitely gradual for each grade. And you learned a little bit more. Every year that that subject came around, you learned a little bit more about it.

Media Literacy

One graduate recalled what she learned from the media literacy class offered in middle school:

In media literacy class we watched videos by these smart people, about the images that we see. We saw things about Disney movies and about the racial stereotypes that are in those. We went through magazines and we picked apart ads, and how they try and relate things to sex . . . like things that don't matter to being beautiful. And they gave us examples from our daily lives. We watched actual commercials that we see at home. We brought in articles that we found. We wrote about different races of people that we see playing what roles on TV, and women, and all that stuff.

It is clear from these comments that students practiced the habits of mind of evidence, connections, viewpoint, and relevance in their class on media literacy to critically analyze how mass media promotes particular standards of beauty, relating to race, class, appearance, and materialism. Marketing directly to children, including commercialization in schools, is also a major industry and cause for serious concern (McLaughlin, 2009; Molnar, 2001, 2005). Mission Hill School staff thought it was well worth the time to offer a class to middle schoolers on thinking critically about messages in the media.

Graduation by Portfolio

Many graduates I interviewed spoke about their experience in preparing and defending their portfolios, a long and arduous process all Mission Hill middle schoolers go through in order to graduate from the 8th grade, and how this process helped to prepare them for high school and college:

> In 7th grade we had to start our portfolios—Portfolios, wow, I never did anything like that before. My portfolio had math, science, reading—I had to read ten books in sixth grade, ten books in seventh grade, and ten books in eighth grade, thirty altogether. And we had to write them down. Mission Hill pushed us through that. It was at that point that I loved reading, from that day on. I'm in high school now, and in another class, the teacher turns around at the board. I take out my book, read a few pages, and put it away real quick. You can't catch me without a book in my hand.

Two parents reflected on the experience of watching their daughter rise to the challenge of solving challenging math problems using linear equations for her math portfolio and defense when math had never been her strongest subject:

> The UN had a figure for certain problems, like food . . . a certain amount of food could save them, and [our daughter] figured out how much money it would cost, and then made a plan for how to get the money, "If one person in every state gave $20 once a month . . . " she did the math for that. And her hunch was, "You pay that much for your cell phone bill once a month." So she really figured out how to make it . . . it wasn't just numbers anymore. This is a person who was not very fond of math.

> This was the first time that math really spoke to her. She got that it could be used in the real world, and it makes a difference. That's one of the things I think is so phenomenal about the portfolios, is that the children are really taught to think and to look at something [in depth], and I also like that within a certain range she was allowed to pick her own subject. And that's what makes the learning so deeply meaningful, because it speaks to her, instead of somebody else saying, "You write a paper about. . . . " And the fact that she had to present it in front of people . . . such a powerful, incredible experience for a student to have.

I asked two graduates what they thought were the most important things, thinking back to 7th and 8th grade, for preparing them to produce high-quality work. They described the power of peer pressure and high expectations:

> Graduate 1: Teachers have this expectation for us, which means that they believe we could do it. And we looked at that, we're like, "What the? . . . We can't do all this work." And then you just do it.
>
> Graduate 2: And then seeing other people do it and being an advisee. And seeing that somebody else can complete this, why can't you complete this yourself? On paper it may seem much more intimidating than when you actually start to get into it and start to do it. And when you become passionate about what you're doing, it doesn't even seem like work anymore. It just seems like, "Okay, I've got to get this done." It's actually kind of fun.

These comments are consistent with Ayers's (2004) argument that children are most strongly motivated by that which is relevant in their lives at the moment, not by planning for their future. In fact, not one of the graduates I interviewed said, "I worked hard because I wanted to go to college or to get a good job." Rather, it was the power of immediate relevance—the power of peer and adult pressure, the examples of peers modeling success and sending the message that success was within reach, and their current interest in the subject matter—that allowed students to rise to the challenge of a very demanding set of tasks.

THE CHALLENGES OF DIFFERENTIATION FOR LEARNERS OF VARIOUS ABILITIES

As many of the statements above demonstrate, one of the unique aspects of the Mission Hill School approach to curriculum is the significant attention given to providing powerful learning opportunities for all students, with their myriad abilities and interests, while not tracking students into rigid ability groups. It is worthwhile to expand on some of the ways teachers strategize about these issues, which can be quite challenging.

One technique used by Mission Hill School teachers is planning interdisciplinary culminating projects to create thematic units that involve many components; only some of the components are required for all students, and others are extensions for students who may rise to a particular challenge. Still, the projects of all students become aesthetically pleasing, artistic, presentable, and the result of hard work. James McGovern, Alphonse Litz, and Jenerra Williams and the graduates speaking about graduation portfolios above, all referred to such projects. The class time planned for these culminating projects generally involved a teaching technique called *critique* and the use of multiple drafts, such as that described by Ron Berger (Berger, 2003; Knoester, 2004).

In such a process, drafts of student work are subjected to a critique involving students and a teacher, which is carefully monitored to include compliments and kind suggestions for improvement for the next draft. This process could be around a student's piece of writing, to-scale model, drawing, or most any other task or product that might be improved with another draft. This teaching technique is also not easy, as a culture of kindness and noncompetitiveness is required for all students to feel safe while their work is being critiqued. The development of this classroom culture must be part of an ongoing curriculum throughout the year. This technique allows students of all abilities to succeed if the culture of the classroom is one of mutual support. Further, teachers plan projects that allow for multiple levels of achievement, allowing some students to complete a larger number of tasks, or to complete the tasks while building on their strengths, which might be a particular knowledge set or a form of intelligence—such as a more visual, musical, verbal, or written approach.

Another way in which Mission Hill teachers think and plan for differentiation in their classrooms is through the more general allowance of choices in the classroom, including giving students a choice of the order of tasks they will complete during a given class period, week, or even longer period of time. Many of the projects and tasks asked of students at Mission Hill School require time to plan—even in the earliest grades, a skill or mindset that Mission Hill School teachers believe is an important life skill. Choice is used within class periods such as math, for example, wherein a teacher may ask the class to work on a set of problems or tasks that require different abilities (such as with the math work previously described by D'Andrea). Teachers generally have to plan in advance several kinds of tasks to be completed during a given period, matched to the various abilities in the classroom. However, instead of assigning students to rigid ability groups, teachers often give students a choice of which task they feel is the "just right" task. I have found that students often choose the same task that the teacher would predict, a task that the student can complete successfully. However, at times, students will surprise the teacher and choose a task the teacher thought was too difficult. The element of choice in this situation allows students the flexibility to take on a greater challenge based on self-assessment. When students choose tasks that are perhaps too easy for them teachers may gently redirect students if this becomes a pattern.

This form of teaching requires more time spent in preparation than simply teaching "one size fits all" from a textbook. But Mission Hill School teachers believe the extra preparation is essential. For example, one challenge teachers face when teaching within an interdisciplinary thematic unit is the difficulty of finding reading material that is at the right reading level for students in the class. This means that teachers are often finding interesting and informative reading material, relevant to the theme, but sometimes having to rewrite it so it is at the appropriate reading level. Or, teachers may create math or science inquiries that are based on the problems "real" scientists may use in a particular physical or natural science theme, adjusting for the skill level of students. These are some of the challenges inherent in creating responsive and challenging curricula for a wide range of learners.

Mission Hill School teachers know the extra work is worth doing since, after all, no curriculum teaches itself. Regardless of the source of curriculum, only teachers can know the particular strengths, weaknesses, interests, and experiences of the students in their classes. Therefore, teachers must be curriculum developers and avoid overconfidence in any published curriculum, although they may be used as a resource. It is with this understanding that Mission Hill School remains committed to teaching diverse students within heterogeneous groupings most of the time and with teacher-developed curricula.

Project-Based Learning Can Support Students with ADD/ADHD

A strong argument can be made that the type of educational approaches common at Mission Hill School, including a large amount of student decision making, with support and structure provided by two adults in each classroom, and long-term projects that involve students planning their time and moving around the classroom and school rather than sitting in a desk for most of the day, are highly amenable to the most commonly diagnosed learning disabilities in schools: Attention Deficit Disorder and Attention Deficit/Hyperactivity Disorder (AAD/ADHD) (Taylor, 2006; U.S. Public Health Service, 2012). Students with ADD/ADHD who often lose focus while sitting at a desk listening to a teacher for a long period of time can find success in performing difficult tasks if given choice and flexibility of physical movement to work on a project over time. This does not mean that these students are not capable of performing highly complex tasks and beautiful and meaningful work, worthy of public praise.

Teachers Working Closely with Learning Specialists

Mission Hill School teachers, many of whom are certified special educators, also work closely with the officially designated special educator at Mission Hill, as well as other specialists, such as the occupational therapist, speech therapist, psychologist, and nurse to include strategies in the classroom that might help particular students to be more successful. Such strategies include using soft weighted pads on a student's shoulders to assist with attention, squeeze balls to handle frustration, or yoga balls to help strengthen important muscle groups rather than sitting on hard classroom furniture. They also may include working on troublesome phonemes in learning to read, or working out a clear behavior plan designed for a student's particular situation. Most of these strategies allow students to spend all of their time in their primary classroom, or, usually on a temporary basis, students meet with specialists in separate rooms. Even when this takes place, often more students meet with specialists than only those with an Individualized Learning Program (IEPs), further blurring the lines between those with "special needs" and those who simply could benefit from a specialist's attention.

POSITIVE EVALUATIONS OF THE CURRICULUM AT MISSION HILL SCHOOL

The Power of Public Speaking

A number of themes arose repeatedly in interviews with graduates and parents about what worked well within the curriculum at Mission Hill School. When asked to reflect on the most important pieces graduates took away from Mission Hill, the most common response—something articulated by almost every parent and graduate interviewed—was the ability and confidence Mission Hill graduates and students had developed in speaking publicly and interacting with adults. For example, one parent said this about her daughter:

> I think one of [my daughter's] challenges all through Mission Hill and has kind of been in her goals every year, was speaking in front of people. So every year there were two [times] . . . that you have to present [before the entire student body] at Friday Share. And you always managed to [speaking to daughter]. And it was just a . . . struggle, and every teacher she had knew it, and she often had them for two years, and it helped her move along, and ran with her through it, and she got to her portfolio and her advisor was her second-grade teacher, who knew her, and knew that whole struggle. And they prepped her, and rehearsed with her, and gave her a pep talk, and she looked inside herself and thought about everything you knew about yourself and figured out you would do it. And she presented powerfully. She wasn't tongue-tied and she fielded questions. And you could see eight years, nine years, depending on the subject, of training all went into that moment. It was really incredible.

Another parent echoed those sentiments:

> I do remember how impressive the 8th-graders were who were taking
> people around when I went touring, that they were very articulate
> and comfortable and sophisticated, and I remember thinking that that
> was really amazing, that that was going to be something that would
> happen for [our daughters], and certainly the efforts to have them be
> presenting or talking in front of other people, I always thought that was
> a remarkable part of the school.

Another parent remarked:

> I just remember that, she was pretty poised in the context of her
> portfolio presentation. We don't get to see that part of her all the time.
> We see more of the little girl part, the whiny part, or the "I don't want
> to do it" or the "I can't do it" part. So it was impressive to see her
> handling that and managing it.

The Habits of Mind

Another theme that emerged repeatedly in the interviews was that graduates seemed to appreciate the focus the Mission Hill School put on the Habits
of Mind, since this way of thinking became useful after graduation in a variety
of settings. For example, one recent graduate said the following when I asked
her if she remembered and used the Mission Hill School Habits of Mind:

> I feel like I use them pretty much every day. In every piece of work we
> use [in high school], I have to use it somewhere. It's kind of natural,
> since I've been doing it for 9 years, they've always . . . even when I was
> younger: "Think of another viewpoint."
> When I talk to people, I use evidence a lot. Because I try to back
> up my opinion with something I really know. And when I'm playing a
> sport, I try to connect it to other sports I've played so it will be easier
> for me to do.

The Focus on Kindness and Noncompetitive Citizenship

A third theme that was repeatedly raised, especially in talking with parents, was the focus on kindness in the school, included in the two school
rules, Work Hard and Be Kind. For example, one parent made this comment:

> I feel like the "work hard, be kind" emphasis is not just lip service, they
> actually . . . play out all the time . . . every day, every hour. And those

two concepts . . . they just honed it down to something the children can work into every situation. And I see the teachers demonstrating it themselves. So in that way, teaching them to be citizens . . . I can't see a more important way, than teaching them the importance of being kind to others, putting yourself in another person's shoes, they do really well at that. And when I talk to parents outside of the school, not in the school—at other schools—or if I know the parent who had a child here and somewhere else, there's a marked difference between the culture of kindness here and at other schools. So I feel like that is done very well.

Two other parents had these comments and stories to tell about the culture of respect and kindness, and the ongoing celebration of cultural diversity at Mission Hill:

To me, it was that it was a community where I knew [my daughter] felt safe, in that there were teachers who I guess complimented . . . [our] parenting . . . they weren't just teaching math or English, they were teaching her how to be a good person in the world . . . and I just so deeply value the connection she made with some of her teachers, which she still holds onto, still holds onto, very deeply. So, that community sense, and those adults looking out for her in a very caring, sort of deeply parental way.

I would just add that she has developed . . . [an] enormous sense of self-esteem, which I think is [partly] due to us and due to who she is . . . [but] is in part due to a school that valued her for who she was. And . . . I definitely think that that was a blessing of that buzzword "diversity"—being in a diverse place. I think she experienced that she was in a school where everybody was different . . . I think it allowed her to hold onto [the idea that] "I don't have to be like everybody else to be accepted." And I think that is a huge gift that [my daughter] carries with her into the world.

Appreciation for the Arts

Another theme that continued to emerge from my conversations with parents and graduates was an appreciation for the attention that the arts received at Mission Hill School. For example, one graduate who attended the Boston Arts Academy (BAA), a pilot high school in the Boston Public Schools, said this:

Well, I think [Mission Hill] was perfect, almost perfect, for BAA because Mission Hill really incorporated the arts into academics. I remember with math: You would be required to do basic mathematics, but the books were more interactive in terms of creating types of games or visualizations to help you solve these problems. When I went to high school, fortunately, it was that same type of process for most of the work.

It was not uncommon for graduates to make statements similar to the following, remembering how many opportunities there were for making music at Mission Hill School:

[Music is] really important. It's a great experience, because at Mission Hill I took clarinet, flute, drums, the recorder, violin . . . they really encouraged it, they really made it possible. They were like, "Whatever you want to take, we'll help you." That's how it is. That's what I really like about the school.

I should add here that it is not true that a student could take whatever instrument he or she wanted to take, although some students took lessons in several instruments. There were times when particular instruments were not offered. However, the school has for many years employed two part-time music teachers, one focusing on strings and another on wind instruments. Students who wish to sign up for an instrument are generally pulled out of their homeroom classes to take a class on their instrument once or twice a week, starting in 2nd grade, and perform their instruments in various ensembles, or solo, for whole-school events.

A full-time visual arts teacher has been employed almost since the school opened, and students in all age groups have scheduled weekly periods to create visual art in the art room along with their entire class, as well as several times throughout the week when individual or small groups of students can sign up to drop in to the art room to either work on an ongoing project or a more temporary art activity.

Theatre is also emphasized at Mission Hill. Although a full-time theatre teacher is not on staff, all teachers plan and direct plays, skits, puppet shows, musicals, and other dramatic arts at various times throughout the year. When a grant became available, the middle school benefited from several years of a professional theatre company producing full-length Shakespearean plays involving every student in the middle school. When the grant ran out, a middle school teacher continued this tradition, but has found it difficult to pull off every year.

The arts constitute an important part of the 8th-grade portfolio process. One graduate recalled:

I remember our [art] portfolio, which was a pain in the [expletive]. You had to think of an art that you were good at. Then you had to come up with a performance. Then you had to talk about one artist. And I felt like that portfolio in itself was really hard, but it was really good. I mean, art is such an important thing. And when we went to [high school], we didn't have any art. And I feel like art is a whole other way of expression.

Many other areas were listed by graduates and parents as strengths of the school's curriculum, including math, writing, in-depth science explorations, general readiness for high school, and others, but the focus on kindness, habits of mind, building confidence to speak publicly, and the school's focus on the arts were the most common responses.

CRITIQUES OF THE SCHOOL'S CURRICULUM

The Curriculum as Too Radical or Non-Traditional

The most common critique of the school's curriculum centered around the perception that it was not demanding or rigorous enough, and especially in the area of math. For example, one graduate, who was heading to college when we spoke, said the following in answer to the question, "Did you feel prepared when you went to high school?"

> Yes. Well, in English and science and all those subjects, yeah. But in math, no, not at all. Because in eighth grade we studied Algebra but it wasn't up to par with the Algebra that they had learned at [the selective private high school he attended]. So I was kind of behind on that. And so what my brother had done, he took Algebra I over again back in ninth grade when he came [to the same private high school from Mission Hill School]. But I just skipped twice and just went straight to Algebra II only partially knowing Algebra I. I think just the workload [at Mission Hill] should be a little bigger, and I think the subjects they were lacking in were math and science. Like science . . . it was a really interesting class but it wasn't the kind of science that you need to know for high school.

I also asked each of the parents I interviewed about the Mission Hill School's refusal to use tracking or grading and whether they thought that was wise. Several parents expressed anxiety about the fact that hierarchies among students were avoided at the school. One parent shared her thinking in this way:

> I think it's a good thing for the kids who underperform. I don't know that it's a great thing for kids who have the potential to overperform. Even saying that makes it sound like other kids don't have the potential

to overperform or be advanced in their work, so the jury's still out on that one. One of the reasons I was drawn to the school was I really was interested in how the working with the different age levels, how that would work. I mean, I was in one mixed class as an elementary kid and I enjoyed it very much, I have good memories from that time. Of course, it was done very differently then, because we third-graders would sit aside while the second-graders were doing their math. So it was still kept very separate in many ways, but yet we did mix some too. I've seen it work; it goes back to the question of "Let's not have any competition." And "Let's not look for kids to do extremely well at something because then it sets them apart from kids who either don't have the parental backing, or, for some reason society has not dealt them the cards that would allow them to excel."

I asked each of the staff members I interviewed whether they thought the math program, which was taught separately from the thematic units using the published curriculum *Investigations* by TERC for the elementary grades and Connected Mathematics Program, developed by researchers at Michigan State University, was a problem at Mission Hill. A majority of staff agreed that it was. I also asked if the main evidence of this problem was the results of standardized tests, which showed that the school was "in need of improvement" in math, and that particular sanctions on the school were possible if there was not improvement, under provisions of the No Child Left Behind law.[2] Several teachers replied that recent test scores were just one piece of evidence.

The Curriculum as Too Traditional or Not Radical Enough

A range of critical comments were made about the school's curriculum as being too traditional. For example, several interviewees stated that the school did not spend enough time focusing on issues of race and racism, even though Mission Hill likely spends far more time focusing on race and racism than most schools. One parent suggested that there was not enough focus given to the arts, and particularly to musical instruments, another area where Mission Hill places a strong emphasis. Another parent suggested a change to the elective classes, which are temporary classes organized toward the end of the year for teachers to offer a weekly class open to the entire school on a topic they are passionate or knowledgeable about but generally in areas not often explored in schools. This parent argued that it sent the wrong message to students: that it's okay to be merely introduced to a topic like knitting. She proposed that instead, once the school offers knitting, there should be opportunities to become more expert at knitting. And there were other criticisms along similar lines about simply being introduced to certain practices rather than becoming seriously focused on them.

Concerns About the Math Program at Mission Hill School

However, the most serious debate taking place at the school, among all of the constituencies interviewed, was about what to do with the math program at Mission Hill School. As indicated in the previous section, a large number of graduates, parents, and teachers shared the belief that since some students report they are not ready for high school math classes, and that some Mission Hill students do not perform particularly well on the math section of the MCAS test, marking the Mission Hill School as one in "need of improvement," that more time should be spent away from the thematic units, which focus on curriculum that is relevant to the lives of students.

Deborah Meier's approach to the problem was quite different from the majority of those who criticized the curriculum:

> I think we were not radical enough. I think we should have kept to what we started to do in the early grades [when the school was first opened] and not gotten involved, even with TERC [the published math curriculum adopted by the Boston Public Schools for all elementary schools, and which Mission Hill adopted in the third year of its existence.]. We should have avoided formal math until the kids were in fourth and fifth grade. We wouldn't have done well then on AYP [Adequate Yearly Progress, a part of No Child Left Behind] either. So, nothing we should have done to make math better probably would have improved our AYP, probably by eighth grade. But as far as I know, [our graduates] pass the MCAS when they get to high school. [But] what we want kids to know about mathematics [for standardized tests] is not what we ought to want them to know. We're not really interested in patterns and games and probability and statistics and, we're not interested in the part of math that I think adults needs to come to terms with. So, that's where the assessment industry and . . . why the world of mathematics ought to be open to all the world, are in conflict. I don't know how to answer that. . . . I think if we were much more radical we would do even worse in the lower grades and even better in the upper grades. Because kids wouldn't be building something they don't understand on top of something else they don't understand.

I asked Meier what a powerful, radical math curriculum would look like. This is how she replied:

> It would be completely informal until kids are about, somewhere around fourth grade. Meaning, we don't do math in terms of written math . . . you just do it as it comes up; we get kids intrigued by the fact that in life . . . there are patterns. We'd have lots of probability

games . . . we'd do some stuff with statistics because it comes up naturally in kids' lives. We'd build on all the math that kids naturally encounter. And we don't try to . . . formalize that into some mathematical format until later, what Connie Kamii was urging us to do [Kamii, 1999]. And then in sixth, seventh, and eighth grade we catch them up with "This is how this is written," "This is how this is said in mathematical language."

Meier explained that in each of the schools she founded she ran into this controversy, and lost the battle of persuasion with her colleagues to adopt a more radical, student-centered, and constructivist approach to mathematics. Although teachers in her schools would experiment with a constructivist approach to math, such as that described by Kamii (1999), when the stress of standardized tests grew, teachers, parents, and administrators repeatedly pressured the school to turn to a published math curriculum, which the school then would adopt.

CRITICAL REFLECTION ON CRITIQUES OF
THE MISSION HILL SCHOOL

What Meier described above is one of the basic conundrums that a school faces when it promotes the development of long-term interests and confidence in math of students, but is faced with pressure from an uncompromising testing regimen that demands continuous improvement in particular sets of knowledge. This happens regardless of whether the knowledge prioritized by the test makers is relevant to the current goals teachers and others who know the students well hold for particular students, including long-range educational goals, such as the development of habits of mind, of identities as engaged students, and of other areas that do not immediately show up on test results.

It is interesting to note that all but two of the graduates with whom I spoke reported that they were doing just as well, if not better, than their peers in high school. Some of the criticisms about the math program at Mission Hill turned out to be exaggerated or even misguided, according to what graduates discovered was expected in high school. For example, one graduate reported:

To be perfectly honest, when I was in eighth grade taking all these standardized tests, I was like, "Mission Hill didn't prepare me blah, blah, blah" . . . and I was really quick to blame Mission Hill. And I did fine on them . . . and I was like, "Oh, I'm really scared now that I'm going to a traditional school," even though [my current selective private high school] is really not a traditional school. But I was like, "Oh, I'm not going to know all the math, I'm not going to know, like, specific history things." I said this in eighth grade before I had come here. But I did fine. I did fine.

Concerns about high-stakes tests and performance in high school are real and must be taken seriously. Still, the question must be asked: What is the cost? What would be lost from what works well at the school in exchange for more intense math instruction from a published curriculum? As I have described throughout this chapter, Mission Hill spends a great deal of energy planning and carrying out a curriculum that is responsive to the ways children are motivated and learn, as well as to the goal of preparing students to participate in a democracy and to be powerful members of their communities. Graduates of Mission Hill School are almost always accepted into one of their top two or three preferred high schools, and 96.2% of the college-age students who responded to my survey had entered college.

Impossible to Prepare for Tests and Produce Lifelong Learners?

Mission Hill staff members believe that what motivates children is the meaning they are making in their explorations, the communities of which they are a part, and the performances or public successes that allow them to develop a strong public academic identity.

There are clearly parents, graduates, and staff that are fearful of the consequences of students being unable to achieve high scores on math tests and unable to adequately use abstract and sophisticated math concepts. While this is an important concern, we must entertain the thought that it may be an impossible compromise to make: to both prepare students to perform well on the math section of the MCAS and to continue to support the ownership students have over their own learning. It may be impossible to both focus on preparation for tests and to focus on helping all students develop strong academic identities at an early age, including counteracting possible negative aspects of the hidden curriculum, such as messages students may receive that they are merely a collection of deficits and unable to use their minds well. I would argue that overvaluing standardized test scores such as those of MCAS often have the effect of sending these harmful messages to students.

The School's Goal Should Be to Produce Lifelong Learners

It is important to critically examine the critique that Mission Hill is not rigorous enough, including statements made by graduates who wished they had learned more, even while a high number of college-age students had gone on to college. But perhaps we should ask, would it be better for gradu-ates to say they were sick and tired from all of their learning? Such a response would suggest their learning time was complete, that they were no longer interested in learning. Perhaps saying they wished they had learned more is a prelude to further study, an attitude that should be welcomed. In fact, I heard several comments that were similar to this statement made by a graduate, which I believe may portray an attitude leading to lifelong learning, rather than expressing relief that their learning time was complete:

> Even after seventh grade, I was like, "Oh, I wish I could do a portfolio on this." Not that I would really ever spend all my free time doing that—Because it's so much work. Like, I remember Sidney Poitier, you know him? . . . Yeah, I wanted to do a portfolio on him when I heard about him and saw one of his movies. I was like, "Wow, I wish I could do a portfolio on him, that's interesting."

When graduates make statements such as this they send the message that, yes, they realize there is a lot they do not know, but they hope to pursue more knowledge in the future. In fact, it is hard to imagine a better attitude for a graduate to take toward learning. There is clearly something powerful about what Mission Hill is doing to produce such graduates. However, it remains to be seen whether it is possible to both produce an attitude such as this among its students while pursuing an educational approach that attempts to teach, from a published curriculum, a great deal of sophisticated material in a short amount of time. It may be wise to consider the critique of scholars such as Kohn (2000) and Ayers (2004), that there is a problem with the common sense conception that learning must be painful and hard and irrelevant to the current interests of students or it isn't learning at all.

Learning Opportunities are Lost when Preparation Is Haphazard

The task of using a more student-centered approach in an urban school with working-class students of color is challenging on many levels. Alphonse Litz critically reflected on this when he said the following in response to my question, "What was the hardest thing about teaching at Mission Hill?"

> One [thing] is when the curriculum emerges from a child, or when we create curriculum in a deep, deep way . . . when I'm thinking [about] project-based learning . . . but really linking it to children's literacy development, [and] their mathematical development—I think [it is important] to be so conscious of . . . taking time to really carefully

think through that curriculum, and have time to build it, and be well provisioned with resources . . . because I think there were some missed opportunities at Mission Hill where it could be haphazard, because curriculum could emerge from a child and it could be deep, but we could miss some things.

As Litz suggests, the Mission Hill School is an imperfect school. Learning opportunities were lost for some students, and teachers may or may not have realized this loss even after it passed. Nevertheless, an appropriate response to missing learning opportunities is not to then try to "cover" all of the material adults want children to know. Rather, it must be to improve the capacities of teachers to understand deeply the content knowledge they teach, and the interests and abilities of their students, so they can find ways for students to see and make more meaningful connections with the material, to solve problems, and to find relevance and meaning in the work.

Changes Made to the Curriculum Should Protect Aspects that Work Well

Damage could be done to the aspects of the curriculum that are viewed most favorably by parents and graduates, such as the school's emphasis on the arts, the demanding portfolio process, and the many ways the students are prepared to be powerful public speakers and create a public identity as engaged students. Therefore, it is reasonable to conclude that the school would be making a mistake by dedicating more time toward teaching to a published math curriculum. It would be worth considering that students would be better served if the math curriculum involved more integration with the project-based curriculum, and dealt with issues (in the form of math problems) that were more clearly relevant to the lives and experiences of students. Graduates reported that they struggled to find relevance and motivation during their math courses in elementary school, but they and their parents were highly impressed and satisfied when they completed their math portfolios.

Math Education Could Become More Meaningful if Modeled after Portfolios

The highlight of the math curriculum in the minds of many graduates was the preparation for, and presentation of, their 8th-grade math portfolios, which involved solving one large multi-step problem, taking a timed test, and presenting this work, in addition to a collection of previous work, before a committee of teachers, parents, a peer, and a community member.

The approach of a more portfolio or exhibition-based math program, adjusted for the developmental level of students, would perhaps be more consistent with the goal of teaching students the Habits of Mind of a democratic citizen, especially the habits of asking "Why is this relevant?" and "How is this connected to something else I know?" allowing students to act on the basis of their answers to these questions. A math curriculum with more flexibility in terms of topics may also allow students to use mathematical reasoning to approach issues of equality and justice, topics that rarely appear in published math curricula, but are highly relevant to the lives of urban youth (Gutstein, 2006), and are also central to the thematic interdisciplinary curriculum taught schoolwide.

While it is possible that a shift toward a more portfolio-based math curriculum would enhance the standardized test scores of Mission Hill School students, I would hope this would not be the primary motivator, but rather that assessment be based on factors such as student engagement, impressive student work, and the ability and willingness of students to create multiple drafts of particular projects, increasing the overall quality and opportunities for public success, a topic to which we will return in the following chapter, focusing on assessing students and their learning.

CONCLUSION

In this chapter I described the pedagogy, including rationale and specific pedagogical approaches, used by teachers at the Mission Hill School, divided by three age or developmental levels. As Apple (1995) has argued, curricula at schools can be divided into hidden and overt messages. The hidden messages to students are not explicitly said or written, but are powerful nevertheless, and may involve the emphasis a school places on quietness and straight lines, for example, the demographic makeup of the staff, or the amount of decision making students are offered regarding their own education. The overt curriculum, on the other hand, is the explicit set of curricular plans and goals, communicated to parents, students, and the community. In this chapter I outlined the overt curricula of rotating 3-month thematic units, supplemented by a published math curriculum, an ongoing curriculum of community building and citizenship education, and a separate middle school curriculum, focusing on the creation and defense of portfolios of student work. The goal of all of these aspects of the curriculum is the development of Habits of Mind for critical thinking, useful for effective participation in a democracy.

In the next chapter I turn to the various ways the staff at Mission Hill School think about and plan for powerful assessment of student learning.

7

Rethinking Assessment

I resist the oversystematization and depersonalization of the school, which threaten to eclipse life on the human and daily scale . . . the ever narrower definition of "normalcy" and the consequent classifying and pathologizing of children.

–Patricia Carini, *Starting Strong*, p. 1

SNAPSHOT OF A PORTFOLIO PRESENTATION

I shuffled along the downstairs hallway of the school, guided by a poised and confident 8th-grader. Acting as a museum guide, the 8th-grader pointed to various works of art hanging on the walls and ruminated on the tools and methods he used to create the work. A small crowd of adults listened intently; they included two teachers, his parents, a community volunteer, and a 7th-grade peer. We were in the midst of evaluating this 8th-grader's combined art and mathematics portfolio presentation. Just moments ago, our group was listening to this same 8th-grader deliver a lengthy talk about his mathematics portfolio. He used a large poster as his visual aid—a symbolic representation of a multi-step linear equation that was the centerpiece of his work. Glancing at large index cards with words he had printed to remind himself of his central points, this young man articulated each of the steps he took in completing this problem, a topic over which we all knew he felt ownership, despite having only recently learned the mathematics. I was impressed with his confidence and fluency of language, something I did not see when he rehearsed his presentation in my classroom earlier in the week. When the presentation of the math and art portfolios were completed, including a summary of papers the student had sent in a packet to each member of the committee 2 weeks ago, he was asked whether he wanted to stay for the committee's deliberations, or leave. He chose to leave. The middle school math teacher shared the results of the timed test, which this student had passed, and the committee began its deliberations. "I was a bit confused by the order of papers in the packet," began one committee member, "but he clearly rose to the occasion and showed mastery with his linear equation." We deliberated for nearly 10 minutes and I took notes for the group. I was delighted to be the one to find the student when the discussion was complete—he had passed his math and art portfolios. A wide grin revealed his relief, and his mother came out of the meeting room and wrapped her arms around him.

In this chapter I focus more closely on the variety of ways that student learning is assessed at Mission Hill School, as well as how those assessments are used and communicated with parents and others.

RECOGNIZING THE LIMITS OF OUR KNOWLEDGE OF HUMAN NATURE

Assessment of children must begin with a particular view of human development, of learning, of the state of knowledge or lack thereof in these areas, and of the forces of inequality and suppression in society, including a critique of how schools have traditionally contributed to that inequality and suppression of growth. At Mission Hill School, teachers approach assessment with great humility—and practice enormous restraint in their judgment—due to a respect for the impossibility of the task of truly knowing the mind of a child. As I wrote in previous chapters in relation to student identity development, a teacher's judgment involves sensitive issues that can dramatically affect how a child sees him- or herself at a young and vulnerable age.

It is worth remembering that in particular moments of candor, even the most well-known "experts" on the brain and of human nature will admit their basic ignorance on these topics. Steven Pinker (1997), in the preface to his book *How the Mind Works*, a finalist for the Pulitzer Prize, wrote:

> We don't know how the mind works—not nearly as well as we understand how the body works. . . . Every idea in [this] book may turn out to be wrong, but that would be progress, because our old ideas were too vapid to be wrong. (p. ix)

Still, as I made clear in previous chapters, the staff at the Mission Hill School, like Pinker, takes particular theories of human development and learning seriously, finding those offered by Dewey, Piaget, and Duckworth, among others, most compelling. But we must ask ourselves, why should teachers and schools pretend to know more about the brain and its development than a leading expert in the field of cognitive science, such as Pinker?[1] In fact, a powerful aura of legitimacy surrounds the educational establishment's measurement of student learning, assigning it a precise number and comparing these numbers, even tying important decisions about a child's future, about a school's ability to operate, and sometimes teachers' pay to these test scores. Mission Hill School staff generally believes these test scores are given too much legitimacy and carry far too much weight.[2]

Today it may be laughable that scientists once measured people's skull cavities to quantify their intelligence. But the clarity about what today's standardized tests are measuring is arguably not far removed in terms of validity from the measurement of people's skulls a century ago (Gould, 1996).

It is impossible to understand Mission Hill School's approach to assessment without first understanding this critique, this political stance of humility regarding the accessibility of a child's mind. This does not mean that there are not powerful ways to know quite a lot about children or how they learn, and that assessing this knowledge is an essential part of educating for democratic citizenship. Since all forms of assessment are limited, however, a wide variety of forms of assessment are needed, and many are used simultaneously at Mission Hill. For example, one teacher summarized her approach as follows:

> I think there has to be a wide range of ongoing assessment. There have to be traditional tests. There have to be observations. There have to be open-ended projects. I mean, it needs to be very, very comprehensive and varied, because information tells you different things.

I begin this chapter with teachers' descriptions of the forms of assessment they use to guide their teaching, often called formative assessments. I end the chapter with a description of the more summative assessments used by the school, which, since they generally take place after something has been studied, are more of a way of assessing the teaching and the school, although they are assessments of students' learning. The best example of summative assessments at the Mission Hill School are the portfolios of student work written and prepared, and then orally defended, by students before a panel of evaluators composed of teachers, parents, a peer, and an outside member of the school community. In Chapter 6 students were quoted at length on their experiences with portfolios; in this chapter portfolios will be described as a form of summative assessment.

Teachers described for me many of their approaches to formative assessments. For example, former Mission Hill teacher and current principal Ayla Gavins described which forms of assessment she thought were most powerful:

> Student work in general I think is the most powerful. It tells so much more than a quiz or a test. The same with . . . if you are teaching kids how to throw a football, watching at recess while they're doing it as they would, I think, tells you a lot.

Laurel McConville, teacher of 7- to 9-year-olds, said this about various forms of assessment she found most useful:

[I use a lot of] anecdotal notes . . . quick check-ins . . . if we finish up something in math, we'll just do a 5-minute assessment . . . [then there's] looking at student work, growth over time, especially with my students that I've had for 2 years. I just love looking at the leaps and bounds that they've made in the year and a half that we've been together, looking at their writing, hearing them read orally as much as possible, running records for reading, taking pictures of their projects and their buildings and asking about them. Math is the one area that we are formalizing this year in terms of assessment, trying to do more monthly small assessments, and then the three bigger—the mid-year, the fall, and the spring end-of-the-year assessments [exams provided by the Boston Public Schools].

The other teacher for 7- to 9-year-olds, Jenerra Williams, described some of her preferred forms of assessment:

I think for me, [it's] our conversations with them. It's hard to document and track conversations, but I feel like that is really one of the most powerful tools for assessing what they know. That, along with when we ask them to put their knowledge to work. "Okay, this is what you know about ancient Greek clothing. Design an outfit for this particular person and make it authentic. It's a woman, she's high in society, and she plays music. Use what you know to produce something."

John Wolfe, a former teacher with Deborah Meier at both Central Park East II and at Mission Hill School, summarized his view of assessment, as well as what he thought was the best way to communicate assessments with parents:

I think the most powerful assessment is the read of a good teacher . . . a good teacher's ability to describe, very precisely, what it is that a kid is doing and has done in the classroom. So I think a really good narrative is the best possible [form of communicating a teacher's assessment]. Now the narrative would include, "I sat down with the kid and administered an informal reading inventory, and this is what I found, and these are the books the kid has read, and here's a sample of a kid's essay about the book," that kind of stuff. I think that's very cumbersome, and takes a lot of time, and it's very, very hard to do well.

I will return to this topic at the end of this chapter as we look more in depth at how Mission Hill School teachers communicated with parents about their assessments of student learning.

Assessments Include Personal Knowledge, Not Only Academic Learning

Assessments of children are not limited to assessing what they do in the classroom. If assessments are to be used to connect with children and help the teacher know how to provide greater learning opportunities, the assessment must include aspects of the child that most educators would not consider "academic," yet can greatly influence the learning of children. Early childhood teacher Kathy D'Andrea explained:

> I think the greatest teachers know that they can learn from her kids, no matter what age, and they listen so intently to all that students have to say. Great teachers not only know their content but they know that that's the third tooth that someone's lost, or the fact that the cousin of a child in your class was shot a year ago on the day. Great teachers see their kids. They take the time to not know what the conversation's going to be about before it starts—that they're true listeners. And they're also trying to walk in the shoes of others, trying to see what it's like for their kids.

Descriptive Review of the Child

There are a number of more formal assessments that all teachers at Mission Hill School carry out each year, which also are used to guide teaching. Among these more formal assessments are the Descriptive Review processes developed at the Prospect Center in North Bennington, Vermont,[3] which Mission Hill teachers regularly conduct during their twice-weekly professional development meetings.

A Descriptive Review is a powerful way of organizing a discussion among adults around a difficult problem. It is based on the premise that teachers have access to a large amount of information about children and the schooling process, but it often helps to gather that information in one place, and to ask oneself questions about the focus of study, such as how the child presents him or herself in various contexts, and to tell that story to colleagues, and then think together about a focusing question. Most often, there is a presenter and a facilitator, along with peer participants. The facilitator ensures that the basic principles of the process are followed. The presenter generally begins the discussion. First, the presenter offers a framing question, to help focus the inquiry. The presenter then describes in vivid detail the person or object of study. If it is a review of a child (as opposed to a review of curricular practice, or children's work, among the many other possible topics or processes), the protocol provides a list of questions the presenter might think about and answer in describing the child, under five headings: physical presence and gesture, disposition and temperament, relationships, interests and passions, and ways of thinking and learning (Himley, 2000).

A child study can also be focused primarily on a particular aspect of a child, such as his or her artwork or writing (a framing question is not usually used in this case). For example, the presenter might present a work of art or an essay written by the child. At this point, all of the participants of the study will describe aspects of this piece, trying to stay as descriptive as possible, rather than diagnostic or conclusive (for example, if a participant notices a shape in a drawing that is round they might say a "sunlike shape," rather than assuming it is a sun). It is also critical that the presenter and participants focus on describing what is there, and not what seems to be missing. The chair will then usually summarize the discussion thus far and restate the framing question. Participants are then invited to ask questions of the presenter. In my experience, questioning begins with clarifying questions, or questions with short answers, meant to fill in gaps of understanding, but are not critical of the practice of the presenter. Participants are then invited to ask probing questions, or questions that may offer suggestions to the presenter, sometimes beginning with the phrase "Have you tried . . . ." or "Have you thought about . . ." Finally, participants are asked to offer suggestions to the presenter, as the presenter listens. The presenter then is given a chance to respond to questions and suggestions. There is often time reserved at the end for participants and presenters to share how the process seemed to work for them, often asking the central question, "Were we respectful of the child and family?"

One of the developers of the Descriptive Review processes, Patricia Carini, best summarized the power of this form of assessment, while also aptly characterizing the limited state of knowledge teachers necessarily have about individual children—a stance shared by Mission Hill School staff, when she wrote:

> Describing I pause, and pausing, attend. Describing requires that I stand back and consider. Describing requires that I not rush to judgment or conclude before I have looked. Describing makes room for something to be fully present. Describing is slow, particular work. I have to set aside familiar categories for classifying and generalizing. I have to stay with the subject of my attention. I have to give it time to speak, to show itself . . . To describe teaches me that the subject of my attention always exceeds what I can see . . . I learn that when I see a lot, I am still seeing only a little and partially. I learn that when others join in, the description is always fuller than what I saw alone. (Carini, 2001, p. 163)

Team of Academic Specialists Meet Weekly

As the example of Descriptive Review suggests, teachers are not alone in their assessments of students at Mission Hill. In addition to carrying out Descriptive Reviews throughout the year, each week a team of specialists meet during lunch time. This group is called the Student Support Team. The team includes the special educator, the occupational therapist, the speech therapist, the social worker, the nurse, and the psychologist. All of these positions are provided by the Boston Public Schools, but since the Mission Hill School is small, these specialists are at the school on a part-time basis. On Wednesday afternoons they gather and speak with teachers one by one on a rotational schedule about any concerns or information they may have about students in their classroom. Specialists carry out their own assessments and judgments, and professional opinions may differ, but this regular meeting time allows all of these educators to share and discuss important information about each student.

Reading Assessments

Other forms of assessment used by teachers at Mission Hill School include practices more or less developed at Mission Hill, and especially by one of the founders of the school, Brenda Engel. Engel developed a form of assessing reading, for example, which involves listening to children read selected texts that were placed at a particular reading level. Teachers ask students to read the text and tape record the reading and ensuing discussion about the text. Teachers take careful notes about the reading and then ask follow-up questions about the text. Teachers then summarize the assessment by marking the highest level of the text the child read with few corrections and that the child was able to show comprehension. There is a cassette tape for each child at Mission Hill that has at least two recordings of the child reading each year. This documentation of children's reading allows staff, parents, and students to analyze progress and growth over time.

Math Assessments

Another form of assessment used at Mission Hill involves teachers interviewing children about math. Engel, assisted by various members of the Mission Hill staff, also developed a set of stages of learning and growth in various strands of math. The math interviews are conducted once a year and allow a teacher to not only ask students to perform various tasks, such as solve math problems on paper, but to see how children use manipulatives, and to probe the mathematical understanding of children by pushing them further if they provide brief answers, or to rephrase questions if students do not at first understand the question. Both the math stages and reading levels of students are noted on reports sent to families, along with much richer long-form descriptions of what the math stages and reading levels mean, examples of student work, and how the Mission Hill School and the teacher approaches these topics. These assessments were developed because the staff value the information gained from these processes as a way to better inform the teacher on how a child understands or misunderstands reading and math work, but also as a way to communicate with families basic areas of competence the teacher sees in the child.

Still, standardized testing has played a growing role in the life of the Mission Hill School, not because school staff has found the tests particularly useful, but because state mandates, tied to strict punishments for noncompliance, have compelled the school to comply with the state testing regimen.

THE POLITICS OF STANDARDIZED TESTING AT MISSION HILL SCHOOL

Standardized tests are administered at the Mission Hill School, but due to the lag in time of receiving test results, the low number of students taking the test at a small school like Mission Hill, the lack of control or deliberation over test items or levels of proficiency, the reductionist view of children encouraged by the tests, and the statistical range of error inherent with standardized tests, they are not the most useful forms of assessment used at the school.

When the school opened in 1997, all Boston Public Schools were required to administer the Massachusetts Comprehensive Assessment System (MCAS) state test for 4th- and 8th-graders in the spring as well as the Stanford 9 test for 3rd- and 4th-graders in the fall. However, this was before the federal No Child Left Behind law was put into effect, and few high-stakes decisions were tied to the test results at that time. Meier was already an outspoken opponent of high-stakes standardized tests (Meier, 2000, 2002; Meier & Wood, 2004). Parents who also opposed standardized testing were sometimes attracted to the school because of Meier's stance, and the parent community at Mission Hill organized and sent out questionnaires to families, asking whether they wanted their child to take the MCAS. If parents marked "no" the school did not administer the test to that child. Since the Mission Hill School was very small, with the large number of parents who asked that the school not administer the test to their child, the number of children who took the test at Mission Hill was small. As a result, Mission Hill School results were not printed in the newspaper, unlike the results of almost all other schools, since anonymity could not be guaranteed. One parent recalled:

It's been an interesting thing with MCAS, because originally almost no one at Mission Hill took the test. You know, when Deb was there. And I was definitely so opposed to standardized testing, especially for young kids. I just hate it. I hate it to this day.

With the arrival of No Child Left Behind, a much greater emphasis was placed on test scores in the Boston Public Schools, as serious consequences were threatened for schools that did not make Adequate Yearly Progress, as defined by schools that reported the test scores of at least 95% of its students, and that students in each cultural subgroup reported gains, among other requirements. Due to increasing pressure from the state, Mission Hill School families were no longer sent notices asking whether they wanted their children tested. Rather, all families were encouraged to have their children participate in the testing. One parent remembered:

Earlier there was this emphasis [at Mission Hill School] on "you don't have to have your kid tested, don't have them tested," and then that had to shift to a "please have your kid tested because the school kind of needs you to have your kids tested." I don't know that much about how that's gone, but I think [the Mission Hill School] may not be seen in the Boston area by the public school officials as being as successful as maybe some of the people whose kids go there. So on paper [the school] doesn't look as strong.

As this parent suggests, once the scores of Mission Hill School students were reported, this became a focal point of both parents and the wider public, since the scores became publicly available, and were tied to real consequences for poor performance. And, as it turned out, the scores of Mission Hill School students were uneven, although generally higher than BPS averages (Boston Public Schools, 2012). It was not long before the test scores became a central concern for the staff as well. I asked each of the staff members to reflect on how this new importance of test scores, as spelled out by the No Child Left Behind Act, has impacted the school. Laurel McConville replied:

Unfortunately, we're in a place where the tests do matter. And so, figuring out how to improve our scores without changing what we do well, making what we do better and stronger, but not giving up our values, or compromising our values, that's a big one, particularly with math right now.

Of course, the MCAS is not used as an assessment in isolation at Mission Hill, but given the great focus it receives in the city and state and across the nation, the tests tend to overshadow other forms of assessment used at Mission Hill. James McGovern expressed his frustration in noticing that the test scores, even at Mission Hill, tended to drown out other forms of assessment used:

> All of the things that we say we want our school to be go right out
> the window when it comes to people looking at [test scores]. I've had
> teachers at our school say, "Of course we look at the whole child," and
> then quote data from a standardized test to say what kids are capable of
> doing. And I've said, "Stop. Listen to what you're doing." And I have,
> frankly, been told to mind my business, that I simply don't understand
> the purpose of assessment. And I find that unfortunate, that people
> feel they're so right, that they've forgotten, to a great extent, why
> Mission Hill School started out with a portfolio process as a graduation
> requirement, why we keep archives of student work from kindergarten
> on up, why the Prospect Center and places like that inspired us to look
> at student work. And I understand the reality of MCAS, and the reality
> of educational culture shifting, but ultimately, I still believe you do
> what you believe is right, and let the pieces fall where they fall.

Various teachers and parents that I interviewed expressed skepticism that it was possible for Mission Hill to both score well on the tests and refrain from "compromising our values." One parent responded to my question of whether the tests challenged the values of the school in this way:

> I think it is [a challenge to the school's values]. Because the purpose
> of Mission Hill, as I see it, is to have each student recognize their own
> particular strengths and to develop them, and that is a very different
> prospect from the standardized test, which is to memorize a certain
> quantity of facts and spew them out. And for a lot of kids, memorizing
> a quantity of facts does not do anything for helping them develop
> their own abilities and strengths. So really the purposes of the test are
> inimical to what Mission Hill is about.

McGovern summarized his opposition to the impact of the tests on Mission Hill with this comment:

> It's one of those games that people play that you can't win. By playing it
> at all, you've already lost. So even if you win the occasional round, just by
> accepting the rules of the game, you've lost something greater. . . . In a
> system like that you have to refuse to play the game or change the rules.
> Otherwise, you're doomed. You end up becoming the thing that you're

striving to fight against. And I feel that pressure. And I know other teachers at our school feel that pressure, and we are not of one mind about how to resolve it or approach it. And that's okay. It's not the first time we haven't agreed.

McGovern suggests in this statement that various teachers at Mission Hill are of different minds on this topic. And I heard a variety of views in my interviews. Several teachers and parents, for example, saw positive aspects of the MCAS. In response to whether the MCAS compromised what Mission Hill values, one teacher I interviewed responded in this way:

I don't think it compromises . . . so again, it gets back to, "What does it mean to be progressive, and truly flexible in your thinking?" You can be creative, you have to be . . . but no, I don't think it compromises it, and yeah, I think it's a good thing, and I think it's important for kids to do well on the MCAS. And I think for, especially as an urban school, for some kids, test scores are access. And so, we are an urban school. And that's important. Now, how you get them to that point, is . . . you need to be really creative around how to get that and still make it a rich educational experience, while at the same time teaching skills they're going to need to have once they leave this sort of oasis.

One parent also expressed her feeling that the test scores mean something important about learning:

I do give some stock to standardized tests. As much as I'd like to say I don't care about them, when I get them, and they're good, and they test well, then I feel like my kids are getting the best of both worlds, because they're still able to pass the standardized tests, and yet they're still getting what Mission Hill has to offer.

I asked teachers whether they thought that the relatively low MCAS scores that some students received in math (as compared with state averages, although not lower than BPS averages) pointed to a real problem with the math program at Mission Hill, or whether these low scores were instead unreliable and merely an artifact of an imperfect test. Several teachers explained that they thought the scores pointed to a real problem with the school's math program. Jenerra Williams, teacher of 7- to 9-year-olds, replied:

No, I think it's real. And as a school, we've acknowledged that . . . okay, this is three years in a row that we haven't done well. And we're on this radar for a reason, and even before MCAS scores were low, though, we knew that there were gaps in our math program, and have been year after year trying to work on it and figure out what do we do? How do we make it better?

Former 7- to 11-year-olds teacher Emily Gasoi noticed that the school's response to the MCAS scores revealed a preexisting insecurity with the math program, since the reaction to the scores has been significant, despite the fact that a small portion of the students took the test as recently as 2007, a topic about which she also wrote an article in the journal *Schools* (Gasoi, 2009):

> I think a big problem with the test [results] is that only 40% of Mission Hill School students were taking it as of 2007, so it's hard to say what the scores would actually be like if they all took it. But I think this is a good example of how the staff is insecure about their math program, because they decided to make some major changes based on these test scores that were not representative of the full student body. But they also do their own assessments, so I think they feel that the kids are not doing as well as they would like in math.

One way the school has responded to the increasing pressure of standardized tests is by including more test preparation in the curriculum—explicitly teaching students how to interpret particular language found in tests, how to strategize about filling in bubbles when time is limited, and how to "think like a testmaker." Some parents viewed this approach as positive and useful, but as one parent expressed, there comes a time when "teaching to the test," and valuing the test results, undermines basic Mission Hill School values, such as combating the "deficit" view of children, and the ranking and sorting that tests are designed to do:

> Parent 1: I really don't think [test prep] should be part of the curriculum. I mean, [I like] the segment that James created about "fooling Stan," or "figuring out how to get past Stan," or whatever, but the problem is that the school exists within a larger context, which is, in essence, hostile to the school's mission. The whole culture is about hierarchy and Mission Hill is all about antihierarchy.

> Parent 2: So perhaps the accomplishment is that it has existed this long and . . . but I think in this environment of economic distress that is also more challenging for the school. They may have less room given to them because of the whole school system being under pressure.

It is clear that the increased pressure from standardized testing is affecting particular practices at the Mission Hill School. Despite the fact that most teachers and parents with whom I spoke lamented the effect of the tests on the school, outside pressures have created or exacerbated insecurities among the staff that may take the school away from the basic values I have described throughout this book. If MCAS scores continue to be less than exemplary and No Child Left Behind continues to be enforced, the school may be increasingly pressured to insert preparation for the tests and an increased focus on textbook math in exchange for the time currently spent allowing students to conduct interdisciplinary projects within the whole-school themes, to play-act in the early childhood classrooms, to build community trust and decision-making skills through the use of community meetings and planning and conducting field trips, to spend time focusing on the arts, and so on.

Since test scores are a concern—and it is not clear to the staff what has to change in order to improve these scores—an increasing amount of time and energy in the classroom, as well as in staff meetings, is spent dedicated to the dubious goal of raising test scores, sending the message to students and parents that this goal trumps the goals set out in the mission statement of the school. As I noted previously, for example, the levels of "proficiency" set by the testmakers are not based on democratic deliberation, and are not made clear to teachers, parents, or students either before or after the test. This alone should cast doubt on the ability of standardized tests to enhance the goal of educating for democratic citizenship. And the notion that testing students at a young and vulnerable age is not likely to lead to stronger academic identities or to stronger test scores for many students in older grades (although this is a primary assumption made by advocates of testing in early grades), is rarely a question for consideration in public discourse on school "accountability," a frequent point made by Meier (2002, 2012), among others.

I turn next to describing how the school approaches communication with parents about student assessment.

PORTFOLIOS AS CHALLENGING CURRICULA AND SUMMATIVE ASSESSMENTS OF STUDENT LEARNING

In Chapter 6 the words of graduates of the Mission Hill School described the powerful impact of the process of preparing and defending at the 7th- and 8th-grade portfolios of student work. Students described how they impressed themselves with the large amount of work they were able to accomplish, they impressed their parents with their ability to present this work in a poised and organized manner, and they impressed themselves and their high school teachers with their preparation for high school work—including preparation for portfolios at the high school level—due to their experience of having gone through a demanding portfolio process before graduating from the Mission Hill School. As one parent said to me in an interview, "If parents [with children in other schools] saw the portfolio process [at Mission Hill School] they would see a rigorous school."

Teachers at the Mission Hill School avoid using the word *rigorous* because it shares roots with the phrase *rigor mortis*. In other words, a rigorous education can be viewed as one that actually kills a child, rather than one that allows her to expand her mind and abilities. So a more accurate way of describing the portfolio processes at the Mission Hill School might be with the words *intense, challenging*, or *demanding*.

Portfolios are part of the curriculum of the school, especially in the 7th and 8th grades, but they are also the primary summative assessment of students at the school. The work completed by students before they graduate constitutes significant evidence, judged by a panel of staff, parents, and community members, that these students have met the goals of the institution. In the portfolios of each academic domain, 7th- and 8th-graders must demonstrate the habits of mind: evidence, connections, conjecture, relevance, and viewpoint—the central aims of education at Mission Hill—while preparing their work for presentation.

However, these portfolios are also personal for the students. As graduates described in Chapter 6, Mission Hill School students complete portfolios that demand enormous amounts of work on the part of the students, but they are also uniquely individualized; each student chooses, within limits, the topics about which they will research and write in each discipline, although there are also elements, such as timed tests, that involve little student choice. The completion and public defense of these portfolios are a powerful way for students to make public a personal identity that combines aspects of home and school identities and interests, while using critical elements of a secondary, academic Discourse (Gee, 1996). This use of portfolios constitutes a way for students to learn knowledge, skills, and dispositions crucial to school success and a more full participation in a democracy, while not viewing students as a collection of deficits, instead, building on what they know, care about, and can do, and pushes students to challenge themselves.

As I have written about in more depth elsewhere (Knoester, 2009), the power of portfolios lies in their attention to the tensions adolescents may be experiencing between their public identities as social actors in a group of peers, and their public identities as students attempting to acquire, learn, or resist, a secondary Discourse powerful in schools. Portfolios create a situation in which it is more difficult for students to say, "School is not for people like me." Rather, students may be more likely to conclude, "Part of who I am is a student, a reader, and a writer; and I can challenge myself at this." And when parents and community members participate in the portfolio presentations, there is no doubt that these students have acquired powerful sets of knowledge and skills.

Heidi Lyne, a former middle school teacher at the Mission Hill School, has written several valuable essays about her experience in organizing and guiding students through the portfolio process at Mission Hill.[4] In one essay, Lyne described her perceptions of how the middle school students she taught presented a renewed focus when it came to preparing for their portfolios:

> The atmosphere in the room changed fairly quickly as we began talking about the upcoming presentations and what they meant. A seriousness appeared in most of the students that I had not noticed in their approach to previous work. No matter how much I had harped on the importance of homework, and doing one's best work always, the general class ethos was to turn in work that seemed haphazardly done and uncared for. This was different. Most of the students began very quickly to care—they asked me to look at things again and again, they didn't groan when I handed things back, they even sometimes went beyond the standards I had set for them. I was thrilled the first time I handed something back saying that it was good enough and heard a child reply, "No, it's not good enough, I want to make it better. I'm going to work on it some more." But this response was not a fluke—I heard it more and more often. As time went on, students began to take more responsibility for their own work. They stayed in for recess and after school voluntarily to work on their portfolios. They were also writing and editing at home and bringing pieces in for me to read. (Lyne, 2010b, p. 4)

Lyne also detailed the challenges she and her first group of students faced, such as the need for students to write multiple drafts, the importance of backing up their work due to lost data, and the difficulty of meeting deadlines to ensure that each member of the various committees received the appropriate materials before the oral defense. Lyne described her impressions after the first group of students presented their portfolios:

> The presentations were almost all both moving and impressive. The students were initially nervous but clearly felt very connected to all the work they had done, and were able to speak easily about it. The parents, too, were both nervous and proud. The mother whose son had not spoken the previous year said, with tears in her eyes, "If you had told me a year ago that my son would be doing this, I would never have believed you." Parents of children who had not seen such a

radical change seemed to feel similarly; some were effusive and some quiet but most of the parents seemed to share a feeling of respect for their children and their children's work. For many it seemed almost a rite of passage; they were seeing a side of their child they had not seen before. (Lyne, 2010b, pp. 8–9)

Lyne aptly titled this essay "Redemption." When portfolios are being defended by 7th- and 8th-graders at Mission Hill, in both the fall and the spring, it is an exciting time at the school, although tense. Every staff member is assigned a 7th- and 8th-grade "advisee," and assists in the students' development of their portfolio, and community members and parents can be seen entering the school to form their committees. There is a feeling that "we are all in this." And the 7th- and 8th-graders know their graduation, promotion, or the requirement of rewrites, and the possibility of spending another year at the school hang in the balance.

With some notable exceptions, at least the first time around, students rise to the occasion and present a collection of substantial and impressive work in each major subject area. After the art portfolio, which effectively transforms the hallways of the school into an art gallery of 7th- and 8th-graders' work, the students put on an art show that also includes performances of poems, raps, dance routines, and songs that is open to the community. It is important for younger students to see what is expected of 7th- and 8th-graders, and what will be expected of them in the future. It is for this reason that each defending student works with a student 1 year younger. This younger student works as an assistant, helping with photocopying and sometimes rehearsing the presentation with the defending student. They also attend the presentation and participate as a member of the committee. If attendance is not possible, these younger students watch videos of portfolio presentations, and look through the work of previous students' portfolios to become familiar with what is expected from this demanding portfolio process.[5]

COMMUNICATION WITH PARENTS AND FAMILIES ABOUT STUDENT ASSESSMENTS

In the years leading up to portfolio presentations there are three formal ways the teachers at the school communicate with parents annually about their children. The first is with two family conferences each year. During these half-hour- to hour-long conferences, teachers, students, and the students' families sit down together. The first conference is held during the first months of the school year and focuses on listening to parents talk about their children. Teachers ask questions and take notes and generally the child is asked to describe the various projects or tasks that he or she has completed or is working on in the classroom. Since time is limited, teachers generally refrain from explaining the entire curricular approach at this time, as this is better done during the family nights. The school also sends out a newsletter each week and includes short passages written by each teacher in the school, describing the various curricular activities taking part in their classrooms. The editorial, or longest column of the newsletter, is usually written by the principal and generally focuses on the whole-school curricular theme and includes a rationale for the way the school is approaching teaching and learning.

The second formal way teachers at the school communicate with individual families is through the use of biannual, or bookend reports. These reports include the results of reading and math assessments conducted by the teacher, and short narrative descriptions of the work the student has been engaged with over the past few months. These reports also include grades, generally in the form of "satisfactory" or "not satisfactory" (the actual words have changed over time) in approximately two dozen categories, spanning from whether the child appears to be practicing the Mission Hill Habits of Mind, to whether the student displays appropriate "habits of work" in the classroom, and is a respectful member of the community.

Finally, teachers write narrative reports for students who have either spent 2 years in their classroom or have an Individualized Education Program (IEP). These narrative reports, as was indicated by John Wolfe previously, are involved and difficult processes, since they are an attempt to communicate with the family that the teacher truly "sees" their child. Of course, parents already know their children very well. The narrative reports focus on the child in the classroom and the school. While including quantitative data, such as reading and math assessment results and an interpretation of those results, they also describe a child's presence in the classroom, social and emotional ways of being, and areas the teacher believes the child should focus on, or areas that are of concern.

I asked each of the parents what they thought of the way the school communicated their assessments with families, including whether it was helpful that Mission Hill School does not use letter grades or tracking. I heard a range of opinions, but this statement I believe represents a widely held view among Mission Hill families:

> It couldn't be better . . . I think letter grades and number grades do
> incredible damage to a community. You know, "George knows he got
> a fifty and then he thinks he's dumb, compared to Alice, who got a
> hundred." I think that's incredibly damaging. And I just think . . . I think
> narratives and that kind of approach to grades is the best way to go.

Another parent responded to the same question I asked above in this way:

> In my view, for my child, yes, it is. And for the community at large,
> I really think it is. It helps us grow as learners, as opposed to ranking
> each other. I know that some parents have had an issue with that. But
> my daughter had some struggles with learning reading, math, et cetera,
> and we were able—with the help of the teachers, and the help of our
> daughter—to hold tight, because she enjoyed those things, and now
> she's doing them. I think that the ranking would have brought her
> spirit down. That grade—that way—would have pushed her someplace
> else that she didn't need to be, and she might have stopped enjoying
> the process and never gotten it.

A minority of parents, however, expressed their wish that the school would communicate their assessments to families using a letter grade, and with more frequent test scores. One parent said the following:

> I wish they would use letter [grades] because you can know what letter
> your child is, like A, B, C, D, like that . . . because you can know if
> your child is a little bit lower than other children. You can push them
> [more].

Another parent expressed a level of confusion that was caused by not receiving more frequent test scores:

> There are . . . very few examinations, and most of those were because
> of outside pressure to give exams. The theme studies are different from
> anything I've known before, incorporating every . . . math, science,
> literature, reading, writing, into a theme . . . [it's] different. And when
> I approached the school at the beginning I really didn't understand
> what that would look like, so it's been a learning thing for me. I feel
> like the parents are asked to have a lot of faith in the school.

One parent appreciated that the school let parents know on what reading level they had assessed their child as well: "I thought that was great. It was incredibly helpful. That proficient, and . . . I forget what it was . . . eight levels. I thought that was fabulous."

Yet, even for parents who said they greatly appreciated the narratives and "bookend" (twice yearly) reports, there was a sentiment that unclear messages were sent from the school about what these assessments meant. For example, on one part of the bookend reports teachers wrote whether particular students "met expectations" in relation to the Habits of Mind and various habits of work. For example, one parent who greatly appreciated the general approach to the way the school communicated with parents also desired greater clarity on these issues:

> I also never understood where the teacher got the information . . .
> When I asked the question I wasn't told, "Oh yeah, we have a list here" [of grade-level benchmarks]. So to me, I don't know if it really is a little bit shaky or it wasn't explained to me well.

It's hard to know how to interpret statements such as these. Depending on descriptive forms of communication with parents, as Mission Hill School does, is perhaps so counterintuitive to what most parents expect that perhaps no amount of explanation about the school's approach could satisfy parents who expect and want this kind of clarity. This brings us back to the place where I began this chapter—the educational establishment in the United States is granted a great deal of legitimacy in assessing student learning, even though the amount of learning that a child achieves is impossible to measure accurately. A school is in a conundrum. On the one hand they must ask parents and the community to trust that they know how to provide rich learning opportunities for their children. On the other hand, if they take a humble approach to assessment and refuse to assign a letter or precise number grade to that learning because they know that number or letter will be granted undue legitimacy, which may also send harmful messages to children, the school appears to some to be undermining its own ability to say, "We know your child and how to best teach him or her."

It is a dilemma, because while parents long for their child's teacher and school to be a crystal ball and have perfect vision of their child's knowledge and growth, as well as what their future holds, this would in fact be a misleading and potentially harmful set of claims to make. Teachers can be highly sensitive and able to see important clues about a child's state of mind, but a humble stance is essential. What the school can promise is to let parents know if serious concerns arise. Both teachers and parents have to learn to trust that their children are capable and able to learn and explore, and that this happens best when their curiosity is stimulated and they are supported in their inquiries and given opportunities to know and learn from knowledgeable, accepting adults.

CONCLUSION

In this chapter I described the approach to student assessment taken by the Mission Hill School. I began with a theory of what is possible to know about the mind of a child, and a critique of the overconfidence placed in standardized testing to understand what children know and are able to do. I described a variety of specific forms of formal and informal assessments, including the Descriptive Review of the Child, running records, tests, and math interviews. I discussed the various points of view of staff and parents of the use of standardized tests at the Mission Hill School, and described the middle school portfolios, which act as both challenging curricula and summative assessments of student learning. Finally, I discussed the various ways that the Mission Hill School communicates with parents and guardians regarding student assessment.

These topics are important to the mission of the school and the goal of educating for democratic citizenship for several reasons. Since the goal of the school is to help students foster the habits of mind needed for critical thinking, teachers must keenly observe their students in a variety of settings and accomplishing a large number of tasks. These observations and other tools of assessment allow teachers, parents, and students the perspective needed to critically reflect on how to improve student learning that is offered to teachers, parents, and students and to help students build on their strengths, foster their identity development as engaged students, and point to areas that need improvement. Assessments such as the portfolio process, that give students significant choice over topics they will study, and require adults to evaluate students based on what they can do rather than based on their deficits, place students in the role of protagonist in their own education. This view of assessment is consistent with education for effective democratic citizenship, as it fosters the voice and decision-making power of students and requires students to confidently interact with adults and others in relatively high-pressure situations.

I turn next to the topic of professional development, or the challenge of creating a culture of critical reflection and growth among teachers at the school.

8

Sustaining a Culture of Teacher Inquiry and Critical Reflection

We must provide for children those kinds of environments which elicit their interests and talents and which deepen their engagement in practice and thought. An environment of loving adults who are themselves alienated from the world around them is an educational vacuum. Adults involved in the world of man and nature bring that world with them to children.

–David Hawkins, *The Informed Vision*, p. 48

LEARNING FROM COLLEAGUES

"What are the deep understandings you are going for?" A colleague pressed me to answer. It was the end of summer and the second day of our staff retreat at the Farm School, a working farm that every Mission Hill School student visits for at least 1 day every year. I was presenting my plans to colleagues for the upcoming thematic unit on government and elections, or Whose Voice Counts? I listed a string of activities I had planned to do with my class that fall. We would read and analyze political cartoons, visit our City Councilor at City Hall, tour the John F. Kennedy Presidential Museum, listen to and watch speeches both recent and historically significant, and then students would research their own political questions and write speeches. Throughout, I would take time to read stories aloud, such as from the book It's Our World Too! *by Philip Hoose about children who became politically active in their communities. The grand finale would be a political convention in which students would present their speeches for guest audiences in our classroom. We would prepare our classroom with red, white, and blue balloons and streamers; students would dress up for the 3-day event and take turns giving their speeches at a real podium with a microphone for our invited guests of students, teachers, and parents; followed by a reception with cookies and juice. When I finished listing my ideas, colleagues provided warm and cool feedback. They encouraged my direction and responded positively to the focus on speeches as a genre.*

They loved the idea of the convention. But there were many suggestions for improvement—suggestions for books and other resources to use, suggestions for additional activities, and various collaborations that might be possible. But it was the deep understanding question that required serious thinking: Why had I thought of this particular set of activities? Had I thought them through?

I began to explain that it was an election year and I wanted my 9- to-11-year-olds to be able to better understand what was going on around them, to perhaps watch a news report and begin to make meaningful connections, to see extensions in their out-of-school lives with what we discussed in class. But I also wanted to introduce the genre of speech writing to students. It would not be the only genre we worked on this fall, but it has particular features and possibilities that are interesting and worth studying in depth. I also wanted to encourage students to be active and involved in our community, to encourage activism and democratic citizenship, and I wanted to present a powerful opportunity for students to make public their engagement with research and politics.

The discussion continued and I wrote copious notes of all of the suggestions offered by colleagues. My teaching at Mission Hill School is public in more ways than I can count, even if my student teacher and I are the only two adults in the classroom. I know the public nature of my work, and the insistence by this professional community to think through, and then to rethink, our practices, makes my teaching more thoughtful and powerful.

In this chapter I describe the culture of teacher inquiry and growth that exists at the school. There is, of course, significant overlap among professional development, assessment, and curriculum. Professional development here means the experiences of Mission Hill School staff to deepen their understanding of all of the subjects I've written about thus far.

KNOWLEDGE USEFUL TO TEACHING IS INFINITE

Learning to teach well in the ways I have described throughout this book involves deep understanding in what I consider four pools of knowledge, which are by nature infinite, necessitating ongoing professional development. These infinite categories are

- deep understanding of content knowledge;
- deep understanding of human nature and how children learn;
- deep understanding of the specific children in your classroom, including their cultural assumptions, and their experiences in the world; and
- deep understanding of self, including your cultural assumptions and particular context in the world, the knowledge and interests you have and can share with others, and how you might be of use to others.

Leading scholars break these pools of knowledge into more finite areas. Darling-Hammond, for example, describes what she believes to be the critical areas of understanding for excellent teaching: subject matter, pedagogical content knowledge, human development, student differences, pedagogical learner knowledge, motivation, learning, how to assess, teaching strategies, curricular resources and technologies, collaboration, and how to analyze and reflect (Darling-Hammond, 1997a, p. 294–297). I do not disagree with her, but believe that all of these can be imbedded in the four infinite pools of knowledge listed above.[1] However, if I were to further break down the four pools above, one dimension that I would add is deep knowledge of systemic inequalities and how these may impact the way teachers view their students, how students view themselves and school, and what is necessary for students to understand and to be prepared to survive—and hopefully work to change—these systems of inequality. The central point here is that teaching well requires deep understanding in multiple areas, suggesting that ongoing professional development is necessary to meaningfully improve teaching and learning over time. A growing number of scholars have examined these crucial issues, although much more work needs to be done (Cochran-Smith & Lytle, 1993, 2009; DuFour, Eaker, & DuFour, 2002; Wenger, 1999; Wenger, McDermott, & Snyder, 2002). Serious challenges arise when designing professional development opportunities for a broad and diverse spectrum of teachers, even when strong commitment to this work is in place. In this chapter I describe various approaches to professional development used at Mission Hill School.

QUALITIES OF A GOOD TEACHER

I began this inquiry into the professional development practices at the Mission Hill School by asking Mission Hill staff about their views of the elements of a good teacher. Meier responded by offering several specific values and views about teachers, children, parents, and the nature of learning:

> [A good teacher is] someone who has a lot of confidence that kids are learners, that they're learning all the time, that their play and their work are not sharply different. . . . Who has a lot of respect for everybody's intelligence, who assumes that the kids make mistakes intellectually—it's not because they're stupid or lazy or trying to get away with something. Who assumes their passions and interests are the most vital things we can work with. Who respects their families, and assumes that their parents are doing the best they possibly can with their children, in the same way that they respect the kids, and who . . . isn't too thin skinned to tolerate feedback that's either from kids, parents, or colleagues that's not always

positive. Who likes to play with ideas, because we want kids to play with ideas and how would you recognize that if you don't do it yourself? Who are decent writers and readers, sufficient for the task. Who have some strong interests themselves. Who have experienced what it's like to really love doing something particular, for which they have high standards. And who has the qualities of looking like they're a laster, they're a person who perseveres, doesn't like to fail, and who enjoys adult company, not just kid company.

What Meier describes above is a lifelong learner and a mentor, someone who could apprentice students pursuing meaningful work and learning. It is a widely held belief that teaching requires deep understanding in multiple areas, but research shows that teachers in the U.S. generally spend a small amount of time and energy on professional development (Darling-Hammond, 2010). This may be due to the belief that all that teachers need to know to be successful can be learned in teacher preparation programs, or are not *learned* at all, but are rather *innate*. These beliefs have been strongly challenged in research literature (Darling-Hammond, 1997a, 1997b; Snow, Griffin, & Burns, 2005).[2]

I do not want to be misinterpreted here. I am not suggesting that teachers come to Mission Hill School unprepared. All teachers at Mission Hill have earned a master's degree in education, for example, and many also have licensure as special educators and/or principals. These additional licenses were strongly encouraged by Meier during the first years of the school, even though she knew that these additional licenses could encourage teachers to leave Mission Hill to pursue other opportunities; Meier saw the ideas practiced at Mission Hill as larger than the school. Furthermore, a stagnant staff cannot practice and demonstrate to students what it means to learn and grow. Teachers must also see themselves as learners, as Meier noted:

> My theory is that a good school should be a provocative place for faculty. That's what professional development is—people bringing to the community dilemmas, problems; they pose problems to each other, and you then take them on in some depth. And you bring in outsiders when you've stumped yourselves, or you think somebody else outside has some marvelous way of approaching this, that might provoke a discussion.

FORMS OF PROFESSIONAL DEVELOPMENT AT MISSION HILL SCHOOL

At Mission Hill School teachers spend at least 5 hours per week outside of the classroom meeting with colleagues. Some of this time is used to make decisions about the entire school, while 3 to 4 of these hours are dedicated specifically to professional development.

Even with a generous amount of time set aside for professional development, the challenge is to create meaningful experiences for adults, even as these same adults are heavily occupied with their teaching.

In each of my interviews with teachers at Mission Hill, I asked how important they thought professional development was to the life of the school. Every teacher interviewed said that professional development was important, although they sometimes pivoted to a description of something they might like to see more of, or change. For example, Alphonse Litz said the following: "I think it's huge. You know, it's huge, but it's again, it's all in the details." Or Roberta Logan, who said this:

> Professional development is a nourishment. So, if you ask me if food
> is important . . . yeah. But there are different kinds of food. There's
> the kind that you eat and chew and swallow, and there's the kind that
> nurtures your spirit, and you definitely need both of those if you're
> going to work in a school.

Partnering with Outside Organizations for Teacher Professional Development

Logan retired from Mission Hill School after teaching in the Boston Public Schools for more than 3 decades. She was known for not only participating in many professional development workshops, but for leading them and writing and publishing curriculum guides for teachers, specifically on the topic of African American history. She worked largely in connection with a local nonprofit organization called Primary Source, which specializes in supporting Boston-area teachers in continuing to learn, grow, and lead other teachers in deepening their understanding of pedagogical content knowledge. Primary Source became an important resource for many Mission Hill School teachers over the years, as most Mission Hill teachers took professional development workshops sponsored by Primary Source at one time or another, particularly those offered in the summer months. During the year Mission Hill teachers often drew upon the substantial library of teaching resources housed at Primary Source.

Mission Hill School teachers also regularly attend and contribute to a number of local and national conferences and workshops. For example, the Mission Hill school staff participates in the Pilot School Share, a conference held each year at a Boston pilot school in which teachers and administrators from various schools offer workshops focusing on teaching and learning. The school then budgets for at least a few teachers (always in groups, so they can discuss) to attend and/or present at each of the following national conferences each year: the Coalition of Essential Schools Fall Forum, held the third week of November; the North Dakota Study Group annual meeting held in February; and the Prospect Center workshops held at various times during the year. These are the most commonly attended conferences and workshops, although teachers have attended many more over the years.

Contrasting Views from Teachers on Effective Forms of Professional Development

Interestingly, various teachers responded differently when I asked what form of professional development worked best for them. Perhaps it should not be surprising that teachers, all of whom have unique interests and passions, as well as various levels of experience and expertise, find different approaches to be more enriching, provocative, or helpful than others. Nevertheless, all Mission Hill teachers expressed commitment to their continual growth, and also understood that they were expected to take some leadership in creating professional development opportunities for their colleagues. When I asked James McGovern about his preferred form of professional development this is how he responded:

> Taking something that teachers really struggle with, based on real experience, and finding a way to stimulate an intense exploration of that subject, whatever it is. Those are my favorite kinds of professional development. Sometimes you just need information. Sometimes they have a curriculum plan, or they have a research project, or something where they just need to get the information out. In which case, that's what you're there to do. You're there to take notes, or you're there to get copies, or you're there to listen to a particular speech or whatever, you walk away, and that's it. But the ones that really take me somewhere are the ongoing ones that exchange ideas . . . that really force you to unpack some of your own stuff along the way, for better or for worse.

Former Mission Hill teacher John Wolfe (who also taught at Central Park East) described one approach he appreciated in exploring critical issues with colleagues:

> Print out a couple of articles and give them to people to read and let them talk about it. I think the best staff development comes when committed staff goes out into the world, sees interesting stuff, and brings it back to the school and talks about it. Mission Hill's thing of teachers in the summertime I think is just brilliant.

Wolfe alludes to a practice at Mission Hill School requiring all teachers to take part in at least 1 week of professional development experiences over the summer. Staff members can choose what they wish to do, but are encouraged to take workshops or make school visits with another colleague, since the exchange of ideas between those colleagues enriches the experience and also better allows the staff members to bring back what was learned. Several teachers echoed the sentiment that this form of professional development was very powerful. Kathy D'Andrea said the following:

> I really love going to conferences and speaking with other people who are either not in schools like mine, or in schools like mine . . . getting out to be with other teachers in a variety of capacities. Then there's Prospect Center [workshops on Descriptive Review], which fill me up every time I walk through the door.
>
> You get readings ahead of time, then they break you up into small groups and you talk about the readings and you use a protocol, and then they also do a piece of art, a piece of kid's work, and you do a Descriptive Review. But then in the evening people bring things to teach, so one teacher taught puppets, making puppets.

Teacher of 9- to-11-year-olds, Nakia Keizer, mentioned that the most powerful forms of professional development for him were seeing other classrooms and hearing teachers talk about their practice, especially if there are video clips or student work to share:

> Visiting other classrooms, visiting other teachers. . . . There are times when I like to hear the theory, that stuff has a place. But a lot of times I like to hear how classroom practice applies, how this stuff plays out. And people have gotten really good at having a balance of those two; here's a video clip of what we were just talking about, of me working with said student on x strategy.

Current Mission Hill principal, Ayla Gavin, described a professional development session led by a Mission Hill teacher, which challenged colleagues to think deeply about analyzing and documenting student work:

> Last night we had a teacher lead us through thinking about documenting student work. And she led us up to a point where we were having this amazing dialogue. And, so, for me that is ideal. It's when we're led to having a really thoughtful dialogue that will follow you. And just the questions . . . it was the thinking that happened during that session that was so wonderful . . . Last night was one of

the best sessions I think we've had all year. It was led by a Mission Hill teacher. There are times when I think it should be led by a staff person and times when someone from the outside should come in.

Former 9- to-11-year-old teacher and current learning coach at another school in Boston, Alphonse Litz, tied his view of professional development to democracy—that a good session is responsive to its constituents, but his view of how this happens stands in contrast to the responses quoted above:

When they were well prepared, like with teaching, when they're well planned, when they emerge from the needs of the participants . . . when you think of good professional development, it's like good teaching and learning. It's just not winging it, "Oh, you know, we got this just this afternoon." To me, that's not good. What is it? For every hour you spend in professional development, there should be 2 to 3 hours of the real planning, or more, 4 hours. And so, when I think of what were good ones? When we were well planned, we presented our work to one another, when we really came out with something. So, it wasn't just a good heady discussion, but saying, "I'm really walking away with this, and this is what I'm going to do in my classroom."

As these statements make clear, different teachers prefer different forms of professional development. While one teacher prefers a highly organized presentation, another prefers a free-wheeling discussion, for example. Contradictions such as these are not easily managed or solved, which may be one reason teachers often resist professional development. The Mission Hill School has addressed this dilemma by offering or requiring a range of professional development activities, some organized by school staff and focusing on a central schoolwide issue, and others tailored to the specific interests or needs of individual teachers.

Peer Review Process at Mission Hill School

In addition to workshops, retreats, meetings, and guest speakers, another form of professional development at Mission Hill is the peer review process, which is both a form of teacher evaluation that leads to promotion or being asked to leave the school, and one-on-one observations and written assessments of teachers. The process involves each teacher being assigned a two-person review team. Teachers are evaluated each of their first 2 years, and if asked to stay at the school, evaluated every 3 years after that. This process is intense for all people involved, but leads to close observations of teaching, to rich dialogue, critical reflection, and often to both broad and specific suggestions on how to improve one's practice. This subject was the topic of former Mission Hill School principal Brian Straughter's doctoral dissertation (Straughter, 2001). In his inquiry of the practice at Mission Hill he found a high degree of collaboration among staff, although he critiqued what he found to be the reticence of teachers to offer highly critical feedback to one another.

The Challenge of Finding Time and the Need to Continually Improve Professional Development

I also heard other critiques about the limitations or problems with professional development at Mission Hill in my interviews. For example, one teacher said the following in response to my question, "What is the hardest part about teaching at Mission Hill?" Jenerra Williams responded in this way:

> Time . . . in a couple of different ways. Enough time to do things, for me personally, enough time to do things well, the way that I define well, which is sometimes too well defined, but the time to do things the way I think they should be done, the time to reflect as often as I would like to, and the time that I miss with my family.

Then there were statements like the following, that at times the planning of the professional development meetings could be lacking, which made the time spent feel even more valuable:

> This is kind of in hindsight, but I thought some of the time that . . . and I think it has to do with one of the flaws of [shared] governance— who's in charge? . . . There were too many Wednesday or Thursday staff meetings where people would gather and look at each other and say, "What are we supposed to talk about?" Something would have fallen through the cracks. And there was, I thought, an over-reliance on math coaches to be the ones to generate the math part of the staff development. And I always thought that was very, very weak. And ultimately I thought it would make more sense for the staff to decide on one thing to explore in depth each year, to the exclusion of every other thing. I thought there was too much that we tried to do.

I asked current principal Ayla Gavins if there were ways that she or the staff offered feedback to those staff members who were leading particular staff development sessions. She described "Little sheets that we turn in to people [facilitators]. It's just real simple. . . . Three questions: praise, polish, and questions" (a practice that began after I left the school). So the issue of the quality of time spent on professional development is clearly on the radar screen of the staff.

CONCLUSION

Gaining knowledge from those infinite pools of knowledge I referenced at the beginning of this chapter is a never-ending task. And the work of a democratic school—to be aware of and counteract the forces of inequality at every turn—requires an enormous amount of effort and knowledge.

It is sometimes said in schools that teachers merely have to know slightly more than their students, and "stay one step ahead." But this view drastically underestimates the difficulty of providing powerful learning opportunities for students. In fact, the more a teacher knows within each of the areas I listed above, the better he or she can show what is interesting about that field, or how to help students see connections to other things they know in order to find meaning and relevance in their work. Further, teachers must know that students don't exist merely as individual biological species, but in a society with powerful forces of inequality that are difficult to understand and counteract, so trying to understand these forces and how they affect the lives of students must also be a subject of ongoing teacher (and student) inquiry. It is not okay for teachers to pretend that all children are the same, for example.

And as discussed previously, in order to build relationships and trust with students, and help students to make connections with subject matter, teachers must be powerful assessors—not just of the mathematical or literacy knowledge of their students—but of their abiding interests, their cultural assumptions, the people and big events in their lives, and many other characteristics of students.

All of these reasons suggest that professional development must be constant and deemed worthy of investments in time and resources. Darling-Hammond (1997a, 1997b, 2010), among others, has shown that teacher knowledge is among the most important characteristics in high-quality, effective schools. Since Mission Hill teachers individually and collaboratively create almost all of their curricula from "scratch" (drawing widely from various resources, including published curricula), professional development is perhaps even more important for them. As perhaps the example of the math program at Mission Hill demonstrates, a published curriculum does not teach itself. It is at best a jumping-off point from where a teacher can communicate and provide experiences that lead to deeper learning.

Teachers are at times lulled into believing that they do not have to have deep knowledge in a content area if they have a published curriculum or set of specific techniques they learned from a colleague. But for all of the reasons delineated above, providing powerful learning opportunities for children re-quires much from a teacher. It is for these reasons that it is perhaps better that teachers at Mission Hill School design their own curricula, often around their own special interests and passions, as this both forces teachers to tailor cur-ricula around their careful assessment of student needs, and allows students to become apprentices to true masters—people passionately in pursuit of new knowledge—even as these masters continue to deepen their knowledge and ability to create powerful learning opportunities for students.

In my interviews with Mission Hill School teachers I found that while all Mission Hill teachers stressed the importance of professional develop-ment and the need to continually think critically about their teaching, their favored ways of doing so varied. While some teachers greatly valued an un-structured discussion about a topic in education or a problem at the school, other teachers preferred a workshop wherein participants learned a specific teaching strategy and walked away with something "practical" to apply in their classroom. Fortunately, since 5 hours per week are set aside for meetings such as these at Mission Hill, in addition to retreats and the requirement (and financial support) to participate in workshops over the summer, Mission Hill School teachers experience a variety of approaches.

Concerns were raised about the use and misuse of time by a majority of teachers interviewed, indicating that this aspect of the school is likely to evolve over time, although, given the differing views of staff members, it is unlikely that an easy solution for how to maximize professional development time for everyone will emerge. Nevertheless, since the goal of educating for democratic citizenship is central to the mission of the Mission Hill School, the modeling of teachers as decision makers within the school is crucial. There-fore, building the capacity among teachers to make the best decisions possible for their students and the school is necessary. Different teachers have differ-ent learning styles or preferences and are at various stages in their careers, but continual growth and development assists in modeling for students how adults play with ideas and treat learning as a lifelong pursuit, and it demon-strates how adults carefully deliberate and use their own habits of mind in leading a school for democratic citizenship.

In the next chapter I conclude with a reflective statement summarizing my findings and analysis, the strengths and limitations of this type of inquiry, and comment further on the important issues raised here.

9

What Does the Future Hold for Mission Hill School?

Fear, despair, and negative valuations of self can be immobilizing, and may keep social actors who have cause to get involved in political contention from participating. Feelings of efficacy, righteous anger, and strength, on the other hand, are more likely to lead one to activism. A first step in movement building in urban schools, then, is to help students appreciate their own value, intelligence, and potential as political actors.

–Jean Anyon, *Radical Possibilities*, p. 179

FINDING GRADUATES

I sat down for scrambled eggs and coffee at Mississippi's restaurant, located in a former brewery down the hill from Mission Hill School. It is a frequent hang-out for the Mission Hill School community. Across the table sat a young man who I had taught ten years previous. It was a joy to see him, and especially to notice how happy and grown up he seemed to be. He still had that toothy smile and dimple I remember from when he was in 4th grade. I asked about his high school and college experiences, about his five- and ten-year goals, and was reminded of why teaching and education matters to real people. He had been across the country and was eager to connect with his "roots," urging me to plan a class reunion. Of course, he agreed to speak with me about his experiences at the Mission Hill School, and I was able to find out so much more about his adventures. My path to this first interview with a graduate of Mission Hill School took turns I had not expected. Having grown up in a world before Facebook, I was planning a wild-goose chase for graduates, involving phone messages and letters stamped with "Return to Sender." But Facebook changed all of that, mercifully. I joined Facebook specifically to track down Mission Hill graduates, and soon discovered that they were almost all on the site—it was like walking into an electronic reunion. The problem lay in whether graduates could step off their rollercoaster worlds to meet me, not whether I could make first contact. Many graduates were in college in far-flung places, but I was fortunate to find enough graduates that had either stayed local or were between their adventures to distant places. Even though I was not able to meet with all of the graduates I would have liked, today I continue to enjoy reading their quirky and often hilarious "status updates," that is, if they agreed to be my Facebook "friend."

Drawing on the voices of 63 people intimately familiar with the Mission Hill School, as well as personal experience at the school, and other sources of information, I have described and analyzed in this book how this unique school approaches educating students for democratic citizenship. I have argued that, because powerful forces of inequality and suppression exist in our society and our schools, a *thickly* democratic school such as the Mission Hill School must be continuously thoughtful, innovative, and courageous in counteracting those forces. Those forces of inequality and suppression are rooted in capitalism, racism, and patriarchy, all of which dehumanize the people who attend and work in schools. As a result, (1) schools are too often culturally insensitive and disrespectful to the diverse constituencies they serve; (2) schools are too often indifferent and unresponsive to the specific desires of their constituencies, especially constituencies of working-class parents of color, when being more responsive (through the use of shared decision making, for example) could elicit a stronger sense of ownership and trust on the part of parents and community members; (3) schools are too often heavily focused on the control of students, causing schools to resemble prisons, especially those urban schools serving Black and economically disadvantaged students; (4) schools too often rely on a reductionist and simplistic view of children, teachers, and schools, placing high value on flawed and misleading tests; and (5) schools too often place little value on the relationship between the teacher and the students—the central relationship at the heart of teaching and learning—investing little trust in the professional knowledge of teachers, and dedicating few resources toward the growth and development of the educational judgment of teachers.

I have outlined in this book how the Mission Hill School has deliberately put in place practices that address the problems listed above by being intentionally inclusive and responsive to the constituencies it serves. I described, using the words of participants, dozens of strategies or practices used in the school—in the areas of community building, decision making, curriculum, assessment, and professional development—to counteract these forces of inequality and suppression in order to create learning environments where students can develop the habits of mind required for powerful participation in a democracy. The strategies or practices range from encouraging student input into their own self-designed curricular projects, to including the voices of parents, teachers, students, and community members at the governing board of the school, which is endowed with the power to hire and fire the principal, approve the budget, and other key decisions about the school. I have also pointed to tensions and problems that have remained or emerged in the process.

REFLECTING ON THE DIFFICULTIES OF CREATING A CULTURALLY INTEGRATED COMMUNITY

In this book I have also described various dilemmas facing the school, about which Mission Hill community members presented various perspectives. These dilemmas have arisen out of the particular sociopolitical context in which the school is situated, and also the principles and values held by parents and staff at the school, even while sharing a commitment to a general vision of democratic education. The first dilemma, discussed in Chapters 5 and 6, related to the contrast between the demographics of the school and the demographics of the most active parents in the family council. Namely, while the school was composed of approximately 20% White or European American students, the parents of these students made up a majority of those who attended the family council meetings, and thus were perceived to disproportionately influence decisions at the school. This contrast was a major concern for many of the staff and parents interviewed, although not all. It is fair to say that this reality concerned more Black parents and staff interviewed than White parents. Early in the school's history a group of parents of students of color was formed to lend a greater voice to parents of color, but it was ended due to concerns by some parents that this would lead to more division rather than inclusion.

Other ways of addressing the racial, cultural, or ideological tensions have included organizing various forums wherein parents and staff were invited to discuss issues of race and class and reach understandings across cultural groups in relation to education and schooling, and utilizing surveys and other means of hearing the voices of a wider range of parents, and not only those who could regularly attend family council meetings. A third way of addressing this issue has been the willingness of the school administration and staff to defend their commitments to heterogeneous classes and other "democratizing" practices of the school, even when parents with cultural capital or economic or racial status feel entitled and emboldened to attempt to attain special treatment for their child, such as grade promotion ahead of their age peers, or other designations of distinction.

This dilemma is important because racial integration is an elusive goal in Boston and across the United States. The Mission Hill School is a unique example of a highly integrated school, so it is worth considering how these racial tensions operate—and to consider whether they are inevitable in a socio-historical context such as Roxbury, Massachusetts. This book offered an opportunity to demonstrate how one school attempts to create space for discussion, mutual understanding, and respect across racial and cultural chasms, although it is unclear at this point whether these tensions might lead to the abandonment or distrust of the school by one or more cultural groups, providing another illustration of why integrated school settings are difficult to maintain. In discussions with Mission Hill School staff since the information for the book was gathered, it appears that the problem of lack of diversity in the family council has markedly improved; however, this issue remains a priority for the school, and as the school has been mandated to move to a different building in the fall of 2012, and to consequently draw from a different geographic area, these issues will continue to be of crucial concern.

Issues of racial and cultural integration are central to the notion of democratic education as I have used it in the framing theories of this book. *Democracy*, in the way that I have used it, is a form of inclusive and responsive community, and it is a way of deliberating around issues of disagreement. The highly charged issues of race and class, where disagreements and tensions arise along racial and class lines, test the capability of a community calling itself democratic to persuade its constituents that it can be inclusive and responsive. Almost all of the parents and staff interviewed agreed that the Mission Hill School was indeed democratic compared with other schools, but the tensions around the family council seemed to test this conception in the minds of many. And it is a dilemma because there are no easy solutions to this question. In fact, some participants, generally White, reported that the racial makeup of the family council meetings was not important to the functioning of the school, while Black participants tended to see this as a significant problem.

DILEMMAS REGARDING THE TEACHING OF MATH AND THE USE OF STANDARDIZED TESTS

The second major dilemma that the school community identified, and about which there were clearly mixed opinions, was the question of how to address the mounting pressure from the state and city to achieve higher results on the MCAS standardized tests, and particularly in the area of math. As one former teacher, Emily Gasoi, wrote in an analysis of test scores at the Mission Hill School (Gasoi, 2009), the definition of AYP (Adequate Yearly Progress) under the federal No Child Left Behind law punishes the Mission Hill School because many parents refused, with encouragement from the school to do so, to allow their children to be tested until recently. My conversations with staff members corroborated Gasoi's analysis that the not-meeting-AYP status pressured teachers of the school to make decisions, especially around the math program, that they probably would not have made had it not been for the tests. The dilemma here is whether the school should change its curriculum in order to achieve higher test scores, even though many of the teachers believe to do so would violate basic principles held by the school staff from the inception of the school. The teachers and parents included in this book expressed a range of views on this issue.

I have argued in this book that the school would be making a mistake by dedicating more time toward teaching to a published math curriculum, risking damage to key features of the school that were viewed as most successful by each of the constituencies interviewed. I argued that the students would be better served if the math curriculum involved more integration with the project-based curriculum, and dealt with issues (in the form of math problems) that were more clearly relevant to the lives and experiences of students. The culmination and favorite aspect of the math curriculum in the minds of many graduates I interviewed was the intense and demanding math portfolio that involved solving one large multi-step problem, taking a timed test, and presenting this work, in addition to a collection of previous work, before a committee of teachers, parents, a peer, and a community member. A significant number of graduates reported that they were understimulated and struggled to find relevance during their math courses from previous years, which were organized around a published curriculum, but they and their parents were highly impressed and satisfied when students completed their math portfolios.

The approach of a more portfolio or exhibition-based math program, adjusted for the developmental levels of students, would be consistent, in my view, with the goal of teaching students the habits of mind of a democratic citizen, especially the habits of asking "Why is this relevant?" and "How is this connected to something else I know?" requiring students to act on the basis of their answers to these questions. Allowing teachers to organize this type of curriculum might also provide students with opportunities to use mathematical reasoning to approach issues of equality and justice, topics that rarely appear in published math curricula, but are highly relevant to the lives of urban youth (Gutstein, 2006). While it is possible that a shift toward a more portfolio-based math curriculum would enhance the standardized test scores of Mission Hill School students, I would hope this was not the primary motivator. This approach would, however, be consistent with the mission statement of the school. Yet, based on my analysis of the interviews conducted for this study, the belief of a critical mass of the current staff is that a greater focus on published math curricula would best enhance the math performance of Mission Hill School students on the MCAS test, and the school appears to be taking steps in that direction.

THE CHALLENGE OF SCHOOL EVALUATION

One of the conundrums of educational research that does not merely rely on the analysis of test score results—due to the multi-faceted and powerful critiques of this way of evaluating learning and judging schools (Au, 2008; Koretz, 2009; Meier & Wood, 2004)—is to find a different set of measurements or assessments that can satisfy the well-justified skepticism held by many that schools can do nothing other than produce and reproduce social inequalities. I have chosen to draw on the narrative reflections of a large group of graduates and parents associated with the school as one way to assess the school. I also conducted a survey of all of the graduates of the school and found that all of these graduates reported being generally well prepared for high school work, and that the Mission Hill School's focus on the habits of mind, and the intensity of the portfolio assessments in 7th and 8th grade, were particularly excellent preparation for high school. I also found, based on a 75.4% response rate of college-age graduates, that 96.2% of college-age graduates reported having entered college. This is compared with a 67% college-going rate for the 93% of students who graduate from high school in the Boston Public Schools (Boston Public Schools, 2012; Center for Collaborative Education, 2006b; Center for Labor Market Studies, 2008), a college-going rate that suggests that Mission Hill graduates are well prepared for later school success.

In Chapter 7 I described the high standards expected and achieved by 7th- and 8th-graders at the Mission Hill School for their portfolio papers, tests, projects, galleries, and presentations. This work is also open to the public for analysis via Lyne's website (Lyne, 2010a) dedicated to this topic, her published essays and analyses, and because on the committee of each portfolio presentation for every 7th- and 8th-grade student sits a community member—or an adult who is not a paid staff member at Mission Hill, nor a parent (although both of these are also on portfolio committees), but is an adult member of the immediate surroundings of the school (Lyne, 2005, 2010a, 2010b). In these senses, the portfolios serve as a forum for "community accountability" and transparency of the high academic standards reached by Mission Hill School students.

These items—the portfolios and indicators of high school and college-going success—are examples of summative assessments of students and graduates of the Mission Hill School. In Chapter 7 I described the formative assessments used by teachers and staff at the school—the assessments used to guide teaching, such as the reading records, math interviews and tests, descriptive reviews, and analyses of student work.

I realize that my description of these assessments may not persuade the most skeptical readers that Mission Hill School holds high standards and teaches its students well, considering the current dominant discourse demands that achievement be described in terms of standardized test scores. For these observers, additional research might include analysis of the work of graduates of Mission Hill School in high school, and might probe deeper into questions of how students of Mission Hill practice the habits of mind in their various pursuits, which prepare them for effective participation in a democratic community. Test scores might be analyzed, in addition to college-going rates, controlled by social factors such as race, class, and (dis)ability. And additional research might compare the Mission Hill School to various other schools to tease out particular features that may contribute most to the educational success of students. These are crucial questions to ask and are not answered easily with the available data.

Nevertheless, the evidence from this study suggests that the graduates of Mission Hill School reach impressively high standards in their academic work. My description of the school here illustrates the practices put in place to address the many challenges facing urban schools, but together create a powerful educational environment. While it is impossible to attribute a college-going rate to a K–8 school, for example, the findings of this study are generally consistent with the findings of David Bensman in his research on the graduates of the previous schools founded by Deborah Meier, the Central Park East elementary and secondary schools (Bensman, 1987, 1994, 1995, 2000). Each of these schools have been shown to defy the odds in many ways, including in terms of graduating urban public school students who go on to achieve a high rate of academic success. The current narrative contributes to this literature by offering a detailed description of key decisions and dilemmas facing students, staff, and parents; and the values and principles that characterize the educational approach at one of these unique schools.

UNANSWERED QUESTIONS ABOUT THE SCHOOL

Throughout this book I have relied on a rich tapestry of voices from people intimately connected with the Mission Hill School. These voices allowed me to draw a nuanced portrait of the school, while illustrating some of the varied opinions and experiences of people intimately familiar with it. The school is imperfect and even contradictory at times. But since these aspects are inevitable in schools, pointing out these nuances is a strength of this methodology, compared with a more reductionist view of school evaluation based on test scores alone, for example, or uncritical praise of a school in all of its aspects.

Nevertheless, there are limitations to this methodology, as with all methodologies. In this case, one limitation is that the school is relatively young, and few graduates of the school have had more than just a few years to reflect on their experiences. It is not clear that the school is sustainable in its counterintuitive and counter-hegemonic approach to curriculum and organization, for example, centered around a conception of education for democratic citizenship and an anti-reductionist view of student achievement and growth. This is especially true in light of the retirement of Deborah Meier, a school leader with strong vision and political clout to defend Mission Hill School practices. These questions may be fruitful areas for future research. How does a school sustain a counter-hegemonic approach to democratic education without the leadership of a well-known founding principal? And perhaps more fundamentally, how might skeptics of the current work of the Mission Hill School interrogate the success of the school? What other forms of assessment might be utilized to judge the work of a democratic school?

These questions are perhaps most pertinent now, since the school has been forced by the school district and city administrators to uproot from its current location in Mission Hill and move approximately 1.5 miles south, into the neighborhood of Jamaica Plain. Along with this move, the school must also increase its size by approximately 40 students, including the addition of a significant number of students who qualify for special education services. My intuition tells me that the school will take on this challenge admirably while staying true to the values and principles articulated in this book. However, if administrators can uproot a successful school from a neighborhood (which is also the namesake of the school) against the strong resistance of the school community, what else can they do? This experience reminds us of the fragility of counter-hegemonic work in education and the importance of building strong community-based movements to support critical educational work.

CONCLUDING THOUGHTS

My Personal Experience with Portfolio-Based Learning

During my own undergraduate college years, in the early 1990s, I was fortunate to be part of a program at St. Olaf College called the Paracollege (or parallel college) that drew more out of me as a learner than any of my previous experiences in school. The program was based on the British system of one-on-one tutorials that were ungraded, but assessed with a narrative report written by the professor. Students were given wide latitude in making choices about their own educational pursuits, including decisions about which books they wanted to read and talk about with professors, and on which topic or question they would like to conduct research. However, in order to graduate from the program, students were required to complete three comprehensive exams and one senior project, and to defend their work before a panel of professors.

The comprehensive exams were generally major research papers and the senior project was often a more creative or artistic rendering of some sort. In my case, for my senior project, I wrote a screenplay based on a novel by John Steinbeck, and directed, produced, and acted in a major theatrical production on campus based on this story. Since I was also becoming certified as a teacher, I then completed a semester of student teaching at a public school in Minneapolis. It was at this time in my life that I read Deborah Meier's (1995) first book, *The Power of Their Ideas,* which had just been published. In this book, Deborah described the progressive educational approach—including the development and oral defenses of student portfolios—of the Central Park East Secondary School (CPESS) in East Harlem, New York. This book resonated deeply with my experience. It did not surprise me, for example, that an unusually high percentage of the CPESS students graduated, and of those who graduated, a high percentage went to college—many more than the New York City norm and the norm for working-class Black and Latino/a students in East Harlem.

Of course, there is much more to the story of CPESS than just the portfolios, but this book set me on a course that would, in a somewhat serendipitous way, allow me to see very intimately what that "much more" was. I found the Mission Hill School, which also developed a powerful form of curriculum and assessment in the way of portfolios, but that tackled so many other educational dilemma for schools, which generally lead to the production and reproduction of social inequalities and suppression of students' creativity and mental and physical health.

The Mission Hill School Looks Different from Traditional Schools

Schools like Mission Hill School were founded for the purpose of pushing boundaries—to interrupt the insensitivity schools generally show to diverse constituencies, to reverse the refusal of schools to listen to the desires and ideas of parents and communities, to stop the suppression of children's creativity via oppressively boring and irrelevant curricula, to discontinue the reductionist way schools view children as numbers in a hierarchy, and the refusal of school systems to trust the judgment—and invest professional development resources in that judgment of teachers. In order to do all of these things, schools like the Mission Hill School look different. The school sometimes looks more like a set of living rooms or play areas rather than desks bolted to the floor, which sometimes makes people uncomfortable, as "progressive education" has been so thoroughly smeared and mischaracterized in educational literature. But schools like Mission Hill School and the Central Park East schools offer interesting case studies of how particular communities formed around principles of democratic education and the interruption of hegemonic forces of inequality. Lessons were learned along the way, and they deserve much more attention and analysis.

Inequalities in Society Lead to Unequal Educational Opportunities and Outcomes

I will, however, end this book on a somewhat somber note. The inequalities we see in schools are pervasive and deeply entrenched in society, and not easily interrupted with a set of educational approaches. I do not believe that very good schools in and of themselves are enough to interrupt the reproduction of inequalities. Disparities among children in many areas, including in the health care, nutrition, and housing they receive, for example, among other economic and social factors, clearly contribute to unequal educational outcomes (Anyon, 2005; Rothstein, 2004). Schools are powerful and important institutions, but even the most inclusive and responsive democratic schools may not be powerful enough to interrupt the harsh realities of inequality and poverty in society. That is why the work of people like Jean Anyon (1997, 2005) is so important. Anyon argues forcefully that the task of truly addressing social inequities requires a social movement to mobilize the resources necessary to make change for children in and out of schools. While I fully endorse this claim, it is nevertheless crucial to give careful thought to ways in which schools can and must help all students flourish and become powerful members of a democracy, including perhaps contributing to the social movements desperately needed to affect significant social change.

APPENDIX A

Methodology for the Study

For the study that provided the information contained in this book, I designed and conducted interviews, surveys, direct observations, document analysis, and practitioner reflection and research to generate data (Bogdan & Biklen, 2006). I then analyzed the data using particular qualitative methods explained here, and finally crafted a portrait of the school (Lawrence-Lightfoot & Hoffman Davis, 1997), organized around central categories, which allow for the greatest explanatory power in describing the ways in which Mission Hill School is unique. A theoretical framework was also developed to further analyze the data and contextualize the themes within the theoretical and conceptual literature on these topics.

SITE AND PARTICIPANTS

I interviewed 63 people intimately associated with the Mission Hill School, roughly one part staff, one part parents, and one part graduates of the school (I say roughly because some staff members were also parents of students at the school). I carefully considered, and consciously attempted to represent the racial and cultural makeup of the teaching staff, parents, and graduates of Mission Hill. Upon gaining the support for the project from the administration of the school, I sent e-mails to staff asking if they would be interested in participating. I also placed an advertisement for my study in the school newsletter, asking parents to participate.

I chose first to survey graduates of Mission Hill School in order to gain some perspective on their views of how their experience at Mission Hill prepared them for later endeavors. I began by sending letters and surveys to all graduates based on the addresses provided by school directories. Upon receiving the survey, I then conducted follow-up interviews with as many of the graduates as possible, based on whether students provided permission and contact information, in order to go beyond the "what happened" questions included in the survey, to probe deeper into the "why do you think that is?" questions, which may be best answered with interviews (please see Appendix B for a list of interview questions). I heard back from a total of

63.9% of the graduates of the school, and 75.4% of the graduates of the school who were college age.

I chose to survey and interview graduates rather than students for several reasons. The first is that graduates had the experience of completing the portfolio process in the 7th and 8th grades, a powerful educational experience that is somewhat unique to Mission Hill School. I also wanted to hear from graduates how they compared the Mission Hill School to their high school and/or college, and whether they felt prepared for high school work upon their graduation from Mission Hill School.

As mentioned previously, the Mission Hill School, located in Roxbury, Massachusetts (but moving 1.5 miles to Jamaica Plain in fall of 2012), serves a student population that reflects the neighborhood in which it is situated. The current demographics of the school are 41.4% Black, 27.8% Hispanic, 22.8% White, 0.6% Asian, 7.4% Mixed or "Other." Elementary school averages in the Boston Public Schools are 33.7% Black, 12.6% White, 43.0% Hispanic, 8.3% Asian, and 2.3% Other (Boston Public Schools, 2012; Massachusetts Department of Elementary and Secondary Education, 2012). Students are admitted to the school by lottery, with the exception of siblings, who are automatically admitted. The percentage of students that qualify for special education services is 24.1%. Mission Hill is a small school, serving approximately 175 students in grades K–8 (a number that will be increasing to approximately 210 in the fall of 2012), and there are eleven "homeroom" teachers, in addition to support staff and student teachers.

I know most of the staff, students, and families chosen for this study well. I taught at the school for 4 years and 6 months, between January and June of 1998, and then from September of 2001 to June of 2005. Upon leaving the school, I kept in touch with many of the students and the school by sending periodic postcards to the school, as well as spending 1 week volunteering at the school in January of 2006 and 2 weeks in June of 2007 before traveling to the school in June of 2008 and January of 2009 to conduct interviews.

I realize that there might be an assumption of bias in my position as a former teacher at the school. This is part of the reason why I chose to interview a large number of people associated with the school, considering the small population size of the school. The choice of who to interview was made based on who responded to my advertisement in the school newsletter, and also who came to the school on the days I was interviewing. However, when particular issues, such as the tensions among participants in the family council, emerged in interviews, sometimes interview participants would recommend talking to other specific parents. I contacted these recommended people, and I believe was able to interview a group that represented a more diverse and representative set of viewpoints.

Each interview lasted from 1 half-hour to 2 hours, although a few were longer. Approximately 90% of the interviews were conducted in person, and recordings and later transcripts were made of each interview. Names of parents and students were changed to protect the anonymity of participants. Real names of teachers and staff at the school were used, if permission was granted.

Questions consisted of a combination of open-ended questions, such as "In what ways is Mission Hill unique?" and "What does Mission Hill do well?" "What do you wish was different about the school?" Questions also asked participants to describe their role in the school and the history of their experience with other schools. More detailed questions focused on the five categories selected that most clearly demonstrated and explained how Mission Hill uniquely approaches and strategizes about central tasks facing schools, including: (1.) building an inclusive community, (2.) decision making at the school, (3.) curriculum, (4.) assessment, and (5.) professional development.

ANALYSIS OF DATA

In analyzing the data, I coded the interviews repeatedly, and constantly compared the codes (Glaser & Strauss, 1967), and wrote memos from which I generated theory that provided the best fit for the data. I also conducted a literature review and developed a theoretical lens through which to interpret the data. Having taught at the school and having read widely in the fields of democratic and critical education before embarking on this project, it was impossible to enter the study without hypotheses of what was happening with my former students, and at Mission Hill School in general. With this in mind, I use many of the methods of grounded theory, while also reading widely across the fields of democratic education and critical theory, using these powerful theoretical lenses to reach a more robust and descriptive evaluation of Mission Hill School.

I used NVivo software to assist in my analysis. After transcribing all of the interviews I uploaded them into NVivo and used these electronic tools to code, make notes, and organize the data.

I created a chart that helped to quantify the number of participants who answered in a particular way to short answer questions. The results of this chart are shared throughout the narrative. Particular quotations were chosen based on a careful consideration of whether the sentiment was a majority or minority opinion, and whether it represented the opinion of more than one person. When conflicting responses were given I represented each of the points of view, if held by more than one person from a particular constituency.

The final write-up of the data and theory was grouped into chapters dedicated to the five major categories I found in my data, with an additional chapter, Chapter 3, dedicated to the specific challenges of opening a new school. I relied on the methodology of portraiture (Lawrence-Lightfoot & Hoffman Davis, 1997) to provide a rich description of the Mission Hill School, paying close attention to the significance of context, voice, relationships, emergent themes, and the aesthetic whole, as described by Lawrence-Lightfoot & Hoffman Davis (1997).

Appendix B

Interview Questions

INTERVIEW QUESTIONS FOR MISSION HILL SCHOOL FOUNDER DEBORAH MEIER

1. How had you originally envisioned Mission Hill School?
2. What made Mission Hill School possible in this context?
3. In what ways did you want Mission Hill School to be the same or different from Central Park East?
4. Were all of the schools you helped to found in New York based on similar principles?
5. Why is democratic decision making, or staff governance, important to you?
6. What was the hardest part about starting Mission Hill School?
7. How might some of the early problems with the school have been prevented?
8. What are the most serious struggles that Mission Hill School faced and continues to face?
9. What is your definition of democracy?
10. Describe how the mission statement of the school was written.
11. Is there a particular population that Mission Hill School best serves? Why? How?
12. Mission Hill has a curriculum that is explicitly about social justice. Why is that important to you? What do you mean by that? Where did the idea originate?
13. Is it important that parents agree with your definition of social justice?
14. How did the Habits of Mind come to be?
15. How can someone assess whether a student or graduate uses the Habits of Mind?
16. What does it mean to be a good democratic citizen?
17. Would the school have failed if a student graduated to be uninterested in politics?
18. What does progressive education mean to you?
19. In what ways does Mission Hill School follow in the progressive tradition?

20. In what ways does Mission Hill School not follow in the progressive tradition?
21. You have been a vocal opponent of high-stakes standardized testing. How does using multiple assessments, or trying to "see the whole child" relate to your view of social justice and democratic education?
22. What are the main purposes of assessment?
23. What are your thoughts about grades given to students?
24. What are your thoughts about tracking and ranking students?
25. Is it possible for schools to interrupt the reproduction of social inequalities?
26. Is teaching a profession?
27. Describe your view of an ideal setting for teacher professional development.
28. What is your view of how teachers become professionals?
29. What is your idea of a great teacher?
30. What is your idea of a great principal?
31. What is your idea of a great superintendent?
32. What is your idea of a great union leader?
33. Richard Stutman, current president of the Boston Teachers Union, has proposed a new type of school he calls "discovery schools," which are a hybrid between pilot and non-pilot schools. They have only some of the autonomies enjoyed by pilots: curriculum and budget, but the hiring rules of non-pilot schools remain intact. Could Mission Hill School be possible in such a setting? How would it make things harder or easier?
34. How much fundraising did you do as principal of Mission Hill School?
35. Is Mission Hill School sustainable? What are its biggest threats?
36. Is Mission Hill School democratic? In what ways?
37. Are there teachers or others who make decisions that you disagree with? What do you do about that?
38. How might Mission Hill School be different if it was a private school, but with a large endowment to defray the costs of those who can't afford tuition?
39. If you were going to start another school, what might you do differently?
40. What does Mission Hill School make possible that other schools say is impossible?
41. Can Mission Hill School be replicated?
42. What do you think is the most common misunderstanding about Mission Hill School?

43. Is Mission Hill School possible only with a powerful, experienced, and charismatic personality at its head, who is able to defend the school from encroaching interests?
44. How can a small school be democratic if the principal has enormously more experience, wisdom, power, and influence than the other members of the democratic unit, and teachers are not given tenure to secure their job placements in the event of political disagreement?

INTERVIEW QUESTIONS FOR MISSION HILL TEACHERS AND CURRENT PRINCIPAL

1. How long have you been at Mission Hill School, and in what capacities?
2. In what other schools have you taught or worked? In what capacities? For how long?
3. What is different about Mission Hill School from the other settings in which you've worked?
4. What is the hardest thing about working at Mission Hill School?
5. Democratic decision making is a key characteristic of Mission Hill School. How does it work? What are its advantages? What are its disadvantages?
6. In what ways have you learned to "do it better," that is, govern democratically?
7. Who makes the decisions at Mission Hill School?
8. What is the role of parents?
9. Mission Hill School has an explicit curriculum, which is, in part, dedicated to "the struggle for justice." What does that mean?
10. Can the Habits of Mind be taught?
11. How do you assess whether the Habits of Mind are being learned?
12. Mission Hill School is known for being part of a tradition of progressive education. What does that mean to you?
13. What evidence do you have that progressive education works better than other theories of learning?
14. Does progressive education work better for some students than for others?
15. How do you teach to the whole range of learners in your classroom?
16. Mission Hill uses a variety of assessment tools, other than tests. What are the key tools you use to assess your students?
17. How do multiple forms of assessment, or "seeing the whole child," relate to your views of social justice?
18. What are your thoughts about grades given to students?

19. What are your thoughts about tracking and ranking students?
20. Is it possible for schools to interrupt the reproduction of societal inequalities? How? To what extent?
21. Describe your view of an ideal form of teacher professional development. How does Mission Hill School compare to your ideal?
22. What is your view of how teachers become professionals?
23. What is your idea of a great teacher?
24. What is your idea of a great principal?
25. What is your idea of a great union president?
26. Richard Stutman of the Boston Teachers Union has proposed a new type of school he calls "discovery schools," which are a hybrid between pilot and non-pilot schools. They have only some of the autonomies enjoyed by pilots: curriculum and budget, but the hiring rules of non-pilot schools remains intact. Could Mission Hill School be possible in such a setting? How would it make things harder or easier?
27. In your view, what would not be possible at Mission Hill School without outside grants?
28. Is Mission Hill School sustainable?
29. Is Mission Hill School democratic? If so, in what ways?
30. Are there teachers or others who make decisions that you disagree with?
31. How might Mission Hill School be different if it was a private school, but with a large endowment to defray the costs of those who can't afford tuition?
32. If you were going to start another school, what might you do differently?
33. What does Mission Hill School make possible that other schools say is impossible?
34. Can Mission Hill School be replicated?
35. What do you think is the most common misunderstanding about Mission Hill School?
36. Is Mission School only possible with a powerful, experienced, and charismatic personality at its head, who is able to defend the school from encroaching interests?
37. How has No Child Left Behind affected Mission Hill School?
38. If someone were to try to replicate Mission Hill School, what advice would you offer?

INTERVIEW QUESTIONS FOR MISSION HILL PARENTS

1. Describe your connection to Mission Hill School.
2. How many years has your child attended Mission Hill School?

3. Has this child, or has another one of your children, ever attended a different school?
4. In what ways is Mission Hill School unique in your experience?
5. What do you like about the school?
6. What do you wish was different?
7. How are decisions made at Mission Hill School?
8. Do you feel listened to by your child's teacher?
9. Do you feel listened to by the school's principal?
10. Do you regularly, or have you ever, attended a Family Council meeting?
11. Do you feel listened to at the Family Council, or among other parents?
12. If the Family Council agrees that they want something to happen at Mission Hill School, does it usually happen? Examples?
13. Would you describe Mission Hill School as democratic? Why or why not?
14. What is your opinion of the school's curriculum?
15. One of the school's three themes each year is entitled The Struggle for Justice (subdivided into: The World of Work, The African American Experience, Who Are We? Where Did We Come From?, and Government and Elections). Do you feel that the school's understanding of justice is the same as yours? How or how not?
16. Mission Hill School is often seen as part of the progressive tradition in schooling. What does that mean to you? Is that something that you generally agree with?
17. Mission Hill School does not use letter grades, student ranking, or tracking. Is that a good thing in your view?
18. How would you describe the quality of communication between you and the school?
19. Do you feel that there is a welcoming parent community at Mission Hill School?
20. How important is a welcoming community to your family and to your child's education?
21. What does Mission Hill School do that you feel either adds or detracts from a sense of community?
22. Was it important for you to send your child(ren) to a culturally integrated school? Why or why not?
23. What do you believe are the greatest challenges faced by the school?

INTERVIEW QUESTIONS FOR MISSION HILL GRADUATES

1. When did you graduate from Mission Hill School?
2. How many years did you attend Mission Hill School?

3. Where have you gone to school since graduating from Mission Hill School?
4. What are your fondest memories from your Mission Hill School days?
5. Do you ever make connections to your Farm School experiences? How?
6. What tasks come to you with ease? Can any be attributed to preparation from Mission Hill School?
7. In what ways did Mission Hill School prepare you well for high school?
8. In what ways did Mission Hill School prepare you well for other endeavors?
9. What tasks are hard for you?
10. Is there anything you wish Mission Hill School had done to better prepare you for later life?
11. Did you form peer relationships at Mission Hill School that continue to thrive? Is there someone you'd like to reconnect with?
12. Do your parents/caregivers keep in touch with other parents/caregivers from the Mission Hill School community?
13. Do you use the Habits of Mind? In what ways?
14. Do you play an instrument?
15. Are you a member of a sports team?
16. What career(s) do you plan to pursue?
17. Do you plan to go to college?
18. Will you be the first person in your family to go to college?
19. Mission Hill School had a curriculum that is, in part, dedicated to looking at "the struggle for justice." What does justice mean to you?
20. Mission Hill School was and is highly racially and economically integrated. How do you think that contributed to your education and experience at Mission Hill School? Do you find similar integration where you attend(ed) high school?
21. Mission Hill School is considered to be a part of the progressive tradition in education. What does that mean to you?
22. Mission Hill School uses many forms of assessment, such as the portfolio process, self-reflections, child studies, reading books onto tape recordings, tests, interviews, and looking at student work, to name a few. What advantages or disadvantages do you believe this has compared to standardized tests?
23. What particular experiences were powerful in your education?
24. How do you think Mission Hill School prepared you to be a citizen in a democracy?
25. What does "democratic citizenship" mean to you?

26. In what ways did going to a culturally integrated school contribute to your education?
27. Are you old enough to vote? Have you ever voted?
28. Have you taken part in student government at your school?
29. In what ways have you been involved in your community?
30. Are you interested in politics? In what ways?

Notes

Introduction

1. This number will increase by approximately 40 students in the fall of 2012.

Chapter 1

1. The response rate of college-age graduates to my survey was 75.4%, so it is possible that the college-going rate of Mission Hill School graduates is significantly lower than 96.2%. However, the college-going rate of Boston Public School students is approximately 67% of the roughly 93% who graduate (Boston Public Schools, 2012; Center for Collaborative Education, 2006b; Center for Labor Market Studies, 2008), suggesting that the college-going rate of Mission Hill School graduates, who have a 100% high school graduation rate, is at least favorable compared with the BPS norm. It may be a stretch to attribute a college-going rate to a K–8 school—many other factors contribute—but this rate is nevertheless a promising indication of Mission Hill School graduates' preparation for further study.

Chapter 2

1. Specifically, Gutmann argues,

> "The principle of nonrepression prevents the state, and any group within it, from using education to restrict rational deliberation of competing conceptions of the good life and the good society. Nonrepression is not a principle of negative freedom. It secures freedom from interference only to the extent that it forbids using education to restrict *rational* deliberation or consideration of different ways of life. Nonrepression is therefore compatible with the use of education to inculcate those character traits, such as honesty, religious toleration, and mutual respect for persons, which serve as foundations for rational deliberation of differing ways of life . . . A second principled limit on legitimate democratic authority, which also follows from the primary value of democratic education, is *non-discrimination*. For democratic education to support conscious *social* reproduction, all educable children must be educated" (Gutmann, 1999, pp. 44–45).

2. The financial collapse of world markets in the fall of 2008, which has been blamed on the deregulation of particular markets, and the enormous government bailouts that ensued, could have, or perhaps should have, elicited a turn in hegemonic

161

thinking regarding deregulation and neoliberalism. However, the financial bailouts and lack of strong regulation on those markets are consistent with neoliberalism's privatization of profits, despite the socialization of losses. And, as previously mentioned, U.S. President Obama has offered billions of dollars in subsidies to states to encourage support for charter schools, which further signals continuity with neoliberal ideology in education (Apple, 2006; Bolick, 2006; Hoff, 2008).

3. Even in the most deregulated, or "open" of school "markets," pressure on schools to perform depends on parental knowledge of school quality. Schneider, Teske, & Marschall (2000) have found this to be a missing component to the "open market" theory since many parents have limited knowledge of school quality.

4. School systems can become so unresponsive and dysfunctional that marketization of schools through vouchers is a rational alternative for parents and students. However, the marketization does not solve the systemic problems of the school system (Apple & Pedroni, 2005; Pedroni, 2007).

5. Most recently, Alexander, 2010.

6. The methodological assumptions of the psychologists cited here, including the ideology of positivism, has been subjected to intense criticism, pointing out serious limitations to these assumptions (Apple, 2004; Habermas, 1971; Teo, 2005). It is nevertheless impossible for educators to operate without a theory of human nature and learning. Therefore, rather than dismissing all psychological theories on these bases and inevitably falling back on hegemonic notions of children as "blank slates," or on behaviorist notions that children can be easily manipulated while ignoring harmful long-range consequences, or on currently popular notions that human behavior is entirely socially constructed, educators and theorists must continue to work in these areas—including being mindful of long-term negative consequences of particular pedagogical decisions, but which may have the short-term effect of raising test scores—taking into account both the biological and socially constructed aspects of children and learning (Knoester, 2011b).

Chapter 3

1. The pilot schools in the Boston Public Schools also conduct an internal assessment of their schools every 5 years, called the School Quality Review. These assessments include a lengthy self-reflection process in which schools must document evidence that they are meeting their stated goals. This is followed by a review process involving outside trained observers who spend time in the school and read the documentation, and share their evaluation with the school and BPS administration (Center for Collaborative Education, 2002, 2006b).

2. A pre-K class was added in the fall of 2012.

Chapter 4

1. In recent years the superintendent of BPS disclosed plans to uproot the school and move it to a different location in the city, potentially threatening the school's relationship with its neighborhood and affecting the demographics of the school. These plans were met with resistance from the Mission Hill School community and supporters, but the move will be finalized in the fall of 2012 (Boston Public Schools, 2012; Guilfoil, 2011; Taber, 2011).

2. According to the Boston Public Schools (2012), during the 2009–2010 school year, 38.9% of the staff at the Mission Hill School identified as Black, 55.6% identified as White, 5.6% identified as Latino/a, and 0% of the staff identified as Asian or Native American, although there have been Asian staff members in the past.

3. An example of school newsletters can be found online at: http://www.missionhillschool.org

4. Around the same time that the school began to hold these public discussions, a book was published entitled *Courageous Conversations about Race*, edited by Glenn Singleton and Curtis Linton. I asked the current principal, Ayla Gavins, whether the idea for "courageous conversations" at Mission Hill came from the book. She replied that it had not. Nevertheless, the book appears to be an excellent resource.

5. As these scholars describe, White middle-class parents are able to influence the schools their children attend using cultural capital that is uniquely at their disposal. An illustration from my own teaching experience at Mission Hill School might be helpful here. At one point the parents of a student in my classroom desired a special distinction for their child: to be placed in a math class a grade above his age peers. Although I tried to ensure the parents that he was being challenged in his current math class, they insisted on a meeting with the principal, to which they brought a math professor from a nearby university to attest to the child's mathematical abilities. When Deborah Meier argued in support of maintaining age-level groupings and keeping the child in his current math class the parents subsequently pulled the child out of the school. Research suggests that cultural capital of parents used in this way would generally result in special accommodations for these students.

Chapter 5

1. Former Mission Hill School teacher Geralyn Bywater McLaughlin wrote a thoughtful and descriptive essay published in the journal *Schools: Studies in Education* about the challenges the school faced when the founding principal of the school, Deborah Meier, decided to move on, and the process the school put in place to hire a new principal (McLaughlin, 2005).

Chapter 6

1. For example, there have been times in the history of the Mission Hill School where particular dynamics among students in the middle school grades necessitated a heavy intervention. One intervention involved the principal of the school, Deborah Meier, after gaining permission and support from parents and all staff members involved, removing three students from their regular middle school classes to complete work with her and others in the school office until the students could "prove" to the adults that they were ready to return to their regular class. They worked in the office for several weeks. In the meantime, the dynamics of the regular classroom changed for the better and the three students were reintegrated, one by one, back into the classroom.

2. The Mission Hill School math average scores are somewhat higher than Boston Public School average scores, and in the older grades Mission Hill School students significantly outperform the BPS average, but this does not prevent sanctions under the No Child Left Behind law (Boston Public School, 2012).

Chapter 7

1. See Teo (2005) for a powerful summary of various critiques of psychological epistemologies.

2. A cursory glance at the history of psychometrics and test creation should throw this tendency under suspicion. It is well documented that the earliest tests of human cognition were loaded with assumptions about race, class, and gender, and tests have been used to "prove" the dominance of one group over another, leading to morally unjustifiable policies such as eugenics, for example (Au, 2008; Gould, 1996; Selden, 1999).

3. I have written in much more detail about this topic elsewhere. See Knoester (2008).

4. Lyne also created a webpage illustrating how portfolios are done at the Mission Hill School, which can be found at: http://gallery.carnegiefoundation.org/collections/castl_k12/hlyne/

5. See Darling-Hammond & Ancess (1994) for an analysis of portfolios at Central Park East Secondary School and Gagnon (2010) for analyses of the portfolio processes of three Boston Public Schools, including that of the Mission Hill School.

Chapter 8

1. The National Board for Professional Teaching Standards (NBPTS), an organization from which I received a certification, has created a list of standards for each certification area. For middle childhood generalist, for example, the standards include: "knowledge of students, knowledge of content and curriculum, learning environment, respect for diversity, instructional resources, meaningful applications of knowledge, multiple paths to knowledge, assessment, family involvement, reflection, contributions to the profession" (NBPTS, 2010). These are also areas of knowledge that I view as imbedded in the four infinite pools of knowledge to which I refer above. It may be important to note here, however, that my certification from NBPTS in no way implies an endorsement from the organization of any of the ideas in this book, although I believe there is significant overlap in values and principles.

2. In recent work, Darling-Hammond (2010) made a comparison between the United States and higher performing countries on international tests and other indicators in terms of the time and expense invested in teacher professional development. She found that Finland, South Korea, and Singapore, among others, invest far more than does the United States in terms of the minimum requirements it takes for teachers to enter the field (and teacher preparation programs are heavily subsidized by the state), the mentorship opportunities available to new teachers, and the percentage of time during a typical school week—more than 50%—that teachers are learning and preparing for teaching rather than directly teaching students. Teachers in the United States generally pay for the entire cost of their training before entering the field, are given a classroom without a mentor immediately upon being hired, rarely have more than 5 hours of professional development per week, and generally participate in professional development activities only after or before the school day.

References

Alexander, M. (2010). *The new Jim Crow: Mass incarceration in the age of colorblindness*. New York: The New Press.

Anyon, J. (1997). *Ghetto schooling: A political economy of urban educational reform*. New York: Teachers College Press.

Anyon, J. (2005). *Radical possibilities: Public policy, urban education, and a new social movement*. New York: Routledge.

Apple, M. W. (1988). *Teachers & texts: A political economy of class & gender relations in education*. New York: Routledge.

Apple, M. W. (1995). *Education and power* (2nd ed.). New York: Routledge.

Apple, M. W. (Ed.). (2003). *The state and the politics of knowledge*. New York: RoutledgeFalmer.

Apple, M. W. (2004). *Ideology & curriculum* (3rd ed.). New York: Routledge.

Apple, M. W. (2006). *Educating the "right" way: Markets, standards, god, and inequality* (2nd ed.). New York: Routledge.

Apple, M. W., Au, W., & Gandin, L. A. (2009). *The Routledge international handbook of critical education*. New York: Routledge.

Apple, M., & Beane, J. (Eds.). (2007). *Democratic schools: Lessons in powerful education* (2nd ed.). Portsmouth, NH: Heinemann.

Apple, M. W., & Pedroni, T. (2005). Conservative alliance building and African American support of vouchers. *Teachers College Record, 107*(9), 2068–2105.

Au, W. (2008). *Unequal by design: High-stakes testing and the standardization of inequality*. New York: Routledge.

Au, W. (2009). *Rethinking multicultural education: Teaching for racial and cultural justice*. Milwaukee, WI: Rethinking Schools.

Ayers, W. (2004). *Teaching the personal and the political: Essays on hope and justice*. New York: Teachers College Press.

Ayers, W., Klonsky, M., & Lyon, G. (Eds.). (2000). *A simple justice: The challenge of small schools*. New York: Teachers College Press.

Banks, J. A., & McGee Banks, C. A. (Eds.). (2009). *Multicultural education: Issues and perspectives* (7th ed.). Hoboken, NJ: Wiley.

Barber, B. (2003). *Strong democracy: Participatory politics for a new age*. Berkeley: University of California Press.

Bensman, D. (1987). *Quality education in the inner city: The story of the Central Park East Schools*. New York: Center for Collaborative Education.

Bensman, D. (1994). *Lives of the graduates of Central Park East Elementary School: Where have they gone? What did they really learn?* New York: National Center for Restructuring Education, Schools, and Teaching.

Bensman, D. (1995). *Learning to think well: Central Park East Secondary School graduates reflect on their high school and college experiences.* New York: National Center for Restructuring Education, Schools, and Teaching.

Bensman, D. (2000). *Central Park East and its graduates: Learning by heart.* New York: Teachers College Press.

Berger, R. (2003). *An ethic of excellence: Building a culture of craftsmanship with students.* Portsmouth, NH: Heinemann.

Bernstein, B. (1977). *Class, codes, and control* (Vol. 3, 2nd ed). London: Routledge.

Blackburn, M., Clark, C., Kenney, L. & Smith, J. (2009). *Acting out! Combating homophobia through teacher activism.* New York: Teachers College Press.

Bogdan, R. C., & Biklen, S. K. (2006). *Qualitative research for education: An introduction to theories and methods* (5th ed.). New York: Pearson Education.

Bolick, C. (2006, June). *Democrats for (school) choice. Wall Street Journal.* Retrieved from http://online.wsj.com/article/SB115094333229787159.html

Boston Public Schools. (2012). *Mission Hill K-8 School.* Retrieved from http://www.bostonpublicschools.org/node/493

Bourdieu, P. (1984). *Distinction: A social critique of the judgment of taste.* Cambridge, MA: Harvard University Press.

Bourdieu, P., & Passeron, J. (1977). *Reproduction in education, society and culture.* London: Sage Publications.

Bowlby, J. (1988). *A secure base: Parent-child attachment and healthy human development.* New York: Basic Books.

Bowlby, J. (2005). *The making and breaking of affectional bonds.* New York: Routledge.

Calvert, J. (1993). *Pandora's box: Corporate power, free trade and Canadian education.* Montreal: Our Schools/Our Selves.

Carini, P. (2001). *Starting strong: A different look at children, schools, and standards.* New York: Teachers College Press.

Carini, P., & Himley, M. (2010). *Jenny's story: Taking the long view of the child.* New York: Teachers College Press.

Center for Collaborative Education. (2002). *Turning points, transforming middle schools: School quality review.* Boston: Author.

Center for Collaborative Education. (2006a). *The essential guide to pilot schools: Overview.* Boston: Author.

Center for Collaborative Education. (2006b). *Progress and promise: Results from the Boston pilot schools.* Boston: Author.

Center for Collaborative Education. (2009). *CCE publications.* Retrieved from http://www.ccebos.org/pubslinks.html#CCE_writers

Center for Labor Market Studies. (2008). *Getting to the finish line: College enrollment and graduation.* Retrieved from http://www.bostonpublicschools.org/files/Getting%20to%20the%20Finish%20Line.pdf

Charney, R. (2002). *Teaching children to care: Classroom management for ethical classroom management and growth* (2nd ed.). Turners Falls, MA: Northeast Foundation for Children.

Chomsky, N. (1980). *Rules and representations.* New York: Columbia University Press.

Chomsky, N. (2002). *On democracy and education.* New York: Routledge.

Clay, M. (2000). *Reading records for classroom teachers.* Portsmouth, NH: Heinneman.

Cochran-Smith, M. (2006). *Stayers, leavers, lovers, and dreamers: Why people teach and why they stay.* 2004 Barbara Biber Lecture. ERIC ED491764.

Cochran-Smith, M., & Lytle, S. (1993). *Inside/outside: Teacher research and knowledge.* New York: Teachers College Press.

Cochran-Smith, M., & Lytle, S. (2009). *Inquiry as stance: Practitioner research in the next generation.* New York: Teachers College Press.

Conger, D. (2005). Within-school segregation in an urban school district. *Educational Evaluation and Policy Analysis, 27*(3), 225–244.

Cooper, B. S., & Sureau, J. (2008). Teacher unions and the politics of fear in labor relations. *Educational Policy, 22*(1), 86–105.

Dahl, R. (1998). *On democracy.* New Haven, CT: Yale University Press.

Dance, L. J. (2002). *Tough fronts: The impact of street culture on schooling.* New York: Routledge.

Darling-Hammond, L. (1997a). *The right to learn: A blueprint for creating schools that work.* San Francisco: Jossey-Bass.

Darling-Hammond, L. (1997b). *Doing what matters most: Investing in quality teaching.* New York: National Commission on Teaching & America's Future.

Darling-Hammond, L. (2010). *The flat world and education: How America's commitment to equity will determine our future.* New York: Teachers College Press.

Darling-Hammond, L., & Ancess, J. (1993). The development of authentic assessment at Central Park East Secondary School. In L. Darling-Hammond (Ed.), *Creating learner-centered accountability* (pp. 49–59). New York: National Center for Restructuring Education, Schools, and Teaching, Teachers College, Columbia University.

Darling-Hammond, L., & Ancess, J. (1994). *Graduation by portfolio at Central Park East Secondary School.* New York: National Center for Restructuring Education, Schools, and Teaching, Teachers College, Columbia University.

Darling-Hammond, L., Ancess, J., & Falk, B. (1995). Graduation by portfolio in Central Park East Secondary School. In *Authentic Assessment in Action* (pp. 21–82): New York: Teachers College Press.

Darder, A., Baltodano, M. P., & Torres, R. D. (2008). *The critical pedagogy reader* (2nd ed.). New York: Routledge.

Davis, A. (2003). *Are prisons obsolete?* New York: Seven Stories Press.

Davis, A. (2005). *Abolition democracy: Beyond prisons, torture and empire.* New York: Open Media.

Delpit, L. (1995). *Other people's children: Cultural conflict in the classroom.* New York: The New Press.

Dewey, J. (1900). *The school and society.* Chicago: University of Chicago Press.

Dewey, J. (1902). *The child and the curriculum.* Chicago: University of Chicago Press.

Dewey, J. (1916). *Democracy and education.* New York: The Free Press.

Dewey, J. (1927). *The public and its problems.* New York: Holt.

Dewey, J. (1938). *Experience & education.* New York: Collier Books.

Duckworth, E. (2007). *The having of wonderful ideas, and other essays* (3rd ed.). New York: Teachers College Press.

DuFour, R., Eaker, R., & DuFour, R. (2002). *Revisiting professional learning communities at work: New insights for improving schools.* Bloomington, IN: Solution Tree.

Engel, B. S. (2005). *Holding values: What we mean by progressive education.* Portsmouth, NH: Heinemann.

Faust, M. A. (1993). "It's not a perfect world": Defining success and failure at Central Park East Secondary School. In R. Donmoyer & R. Kos (Eds.), *At-risk students: Portraits, policies, programs, and practices* (pp. 323–367). Albany: State University of New York.

Fine, M. (1991). *Framing dropouts: Notes on the politics of an urban public high school.* Albany: SUNY Press.

Finn, C., Manno, B., & Vanourek, G. (2001). *Charter schools in action: renewing public education.* Princeton, NJ: Princeton University Press.

Fodor, J. (1982). *The modularity of mind.* Cambridge, MA: MIT Press.

Foner, E. (1998). *The story of American freedom.* New York: W.W. Norton & Co.

Formisano, R. (2004). *Boston against busing: Race, class, and ethnicity in the 1960s and 1970s.* Chapel Hill: University of North Carolina Press.

Freire, P. (1970). *Pedagogy of the oppressed.* New York: Continuum.

Freire, P. (1974). *Education for critical consciousness.* New York: Continuum.

Freire, P. (1995). *Letters to Cristina: Reflections on my life and work.* New York: Routledge.

Freire, P. (2005). *Teachers as cultural workers: Letters to those who dare teach.* Boulder, CO: Westview Press.

Froebel, F. (2005). *The education of man.* Mineola, NY: Dover Publications.

Gagnon, L. (2010). *Ready for the future: The role of performance assessments in shaping graduates' academic, professional, and personal lives.* Boston: Center for Collaborative Education.

Gardner, H. (1983). *Frames of mind: The theory of multiple intelligences.* New York: Basic Books.

Gasoi, E. (2009). How we define success: Holding values in an era of high stakes accountability. *Schools: Studies in Education, 6*(2), 173–186.

Gasoi, E. (2011). Emily Gasoi. In S. Chaltain (Ed.), *Faces of learning: 50 powerful stories of defining moments in education* (pp. 70–72). San Francisco: Jossey-Bass.

Gasoi, E. (2012). *Active accountability: A cross-case study of two schools negotiating improvement, change, and organizational integrity* (Unpublished doctoral dissertation). Unversity of Pennsylvania, Philadelphia, PA.

Gavins, A. (2005). Being on a moving train. In S. Nieto (Ed.), *Why we teach* (pp. 97–104). New York: Teachers College Press.

Gay, G. (2010). Culturally responsive teaching: Theory, research, and practice (2nd ed.). New York: Teachers College Press.

Gee, J. P. (1996). *Social linguistics and literacies: Ideology in discourses* (2nd ed.). New York: RoutledgeFalmer.

Gee, J. P. (2004). *Situated language and learning: A critique of traditional schooling.* New York: Routledge.

Gilligan, C., & Richards, D. (2008). *The deepening darkness: Patriarchy, resistance & democacy's future*. Cambridge, UK: Cambridge University Press.

Giroux, H. (1988). *Teachers as intellectuals*. South Hadley, MA: Bergin & Garvin.

Giroux, H. (2001). *Theory and resistance in education*. Santa Barbara, CA: Praeger.

Glaser, B. (1978). *Theoretical sensitivity*. Mill Valley, CA: Sociology Press.

Glaser, B., & Strauss, A. (1967). *The discovery of grounded theory: Strategies for qualitative research*. New Brunswick, NJ: Adline Transaction.

Gomes, C. F., & Unger, R. M. (1996). *The next step: A practical alternative to neoliberalism*. Madison, WI: Global Studies Research Program.

Gould, S. J. (1996*). The mismeasure of man*. New York: W.W. Norton & Co.

Graff, G. (2003). *Clueless in academe*. New Haven, CT: Yale University Press.

Gramsci, A. (1971). *Selections from the prison notebooks*. New York: International Publishers.

Grant, C. A., & Gomez, M. L. (Eds.). (2001). *Campus and classroom: Making schooling multicultural* (2nd ed.). Upper Saddle River, NJ: Merrill/Prentice.

Guilfoil, J. M. (2011, November 15). Mission Hill School parents want school to stay. *Boston Globe*. Retreived from http://www.bostonglobe.com/metro/2011/11/15/parents-want-mission-hill-school-stay/rRJNXM3ZW3S7Nng-ZoIu5pO/story.html

Gutmann, A. (1999). *Democratic education*. Princeton, NJ: Princeton University Press.

Gutstein, E. (2006). *Reading and writing the world with mathematics: Toward a pedagogy for social justice*. New York: Routledge.

Habermas, J. (1971). *Knowledge and human interests*. Boston: Beacon Press.

Harvey, D. (2005). *A brief history of neoliberalism*. New York: Oxford University Press.

Hawkins, D. (1974). *The informed vision: Essays on learning and human nature*. New York: Agathon Press.

Hillson, J. (1977). *The battle of Boston*. New York: Pathfinder Press.

Himley, M. (2000). *From another angle: Children's strengths and school standards*. New York: Teachers College Press.

Hoff, D. J. (2008, September 17). McCain, Obama spar on education. *Education Week*, p. 6.

hooks, b. (1994). *Teaching to transgress: Education as the practice of freedom*. New York: Routledge.

Hoose, P. M. (2002). *It's our world too!: Young people who are making a difference*. New York: Farrar, Straus and Giroux.

Horvat, E. M., Weininger, E., & Lareau, A. (2003). From social ties to social capital: Class differences in the relations between schools and parent networks. *American Educational Research Journal, 40*(2), 319–351.

Ingersoll, R. (1995). *Teacher supply, teacher quality, and teacher turnover*. Washington, DC: National Center for Educational Statistics.

Ingersoll, R. (2003). *Why do high-poverty schools have difficulty staffing their classrooms with qualified teachers?* Washington, DC: Renewing Our Schools, Securing Our Future, A National Task Force on Public Education. Retrieved from http://www.americanprogress.org/kf/ingersoll-final.pdf

Jan, T. (2007, November 9). High-flying pilot schools: Study points to range of successes in Boston's experimental program. *Boston Globe.* Retreived from http://www.boston.com/news/education/k_12/mcas/articles/2007/11/09/high_flying_pilot_schools/?page=full

Johnson, D. D., & Johnson, B. (2006). *High stakes: Poverty, testing, and failure in American schools* (2nd ed.). Lanham, MD: Rowman & Littlefield.

Johnson, S. M., & Landman, J. (2000). Sometimes bureaucracy has its charms: The working conditions of teachers in deregulated schools. *Teachers College Record, 102*(1), pp. 85–124.

Johnson, S. M., & The Project on the Next Generation of Teachers. (2004). *Finders and keepers: Helping new teachers survive and thrive in our schools.* San Francisco: Jossey-Bass.

Kahlenberg. R. D. (2006). The history of collective bargaining among teachers. In J. Hannaway & A. J. Rotherham (eds.), *Collective bargaining in education: Negotiating change in today's schools* (pp. 27–52). Cambridge, MA: Harvard Education Press.

Kamii, C. (1999). *Young children reinvent mathematics: Implications of Piaget's theory* (2nd ed.). New York: Teachers College Press.

Knoester, M. (2003). Education according to Chomsky. *Mind, Culture, and Activity, 10*(3), 266–270.

Knoester, M. (2004). Eavesdropping on Ron Berger's classroom. *Schools: Studies in Education, 1*(2), 166–170.

Knoester, M. (2008). Learning to describe, describing to understand. *Schools: Studies in Education, 5*(1), 146–55.

Knoester, M. (2009, May). Inquiry into urban adolescent independent reading habits: Can Gee's theory of Discourses provide insight? *Journal of Adolescent & Adult Literacy, 52*(8), 676–85.

Knoester, M. (2010). Independent reading and the "social turn": How adolescent reading habits and motivation may be related to cultivating social relationships. *Networks: An Online Journal for Teacher Research.* Retrieved from http://journals.library.wisc.edu/index.php/networks

Knoester, M. (2011a). Is the outcry for more pilot schools warranted? Democracy, collective bargaining, deregulation, and the politics of school reform in Boston. *Educational Policy, 25*(3), 387–423.

Knoester, M. (2011b). Who will benefit from the "sociocultural turn" in education? *Pedagogy, Culture & Society, 19*(2), 311–318.

Knoester, M. (Ed.). (2012). *International struggles for critical democratic education.* New York: Peter Lang.

Kohl, H. (1995). *I won't learn from you: And other thoughts on creative maladjustment.* New York: New Press.

Kohn, A. (1999). *The schools our children deserve: Moving beyond traditional classrooms and "tougher standards."* Boston: Houghton Mifflin.

Kohn, A. (2000). *The case against standardized testing: Raising the scores, ruining the schools.* Portsmouth, NH: Heinemann.

Koretz, D. M. (2009). *Measuring up: What educational testing really tells us.* Cambridge, MA: Harvard University Press.

Kozol, J. (1967). *Death at an early age.* Boston: Houghton Mifflin.

Kozol, J. (1992). *Savage inequalities: Children in America's schools.* New York: Harper Perennial.

Kozol. J. (2005). *The shame of the nation: The restoration of apartheid schooling in America.* New York: Crown Publishers.

Ladson-Billings, G. (2006). *The dreamkeepers: Successful teachers of African American children* (2nd ed.). San Francisco: Jossey-Bass.

Ladson-Billings, G. (1995). Toward a theory of culturally relevant pedagogy. *American Educational Research Journal, 32*(3), 465–491.

Lappe, F. M. (2005). *Democracy's edge.* San Francisco: Jossey-Bass.

Lappe, F. M., & Du Bois, P. M. (1994). *The quickening of America.* San Francisco: Jossey-Bass.

Lareau, A., & Horvat, E. M. (1999). Moments of social inclusion and exclusion: Race, class and cultural capital in family-school relationships. *Sociology of Education, 72*(1), 37–53.

Lawrence-Lightfoot, S. (2003). *The essential conversation: What parents and teachers can learn from each other.* New York: Ballantine Books.

Lawrence-Lightfoot, S., & Hoffman Davis, J. (1997). *The art and science of portraiture.* San Francisco: Jossey-Bass.

Lipman, P. (1998). *Race, class, and power in school restructuring.* New York: State University of New York Press.

Lipman, P. (2004). *High stakes education.* New York: Routledge.

Lubienski, C. (2003). Instrumentalist perspectives on the "public" in public education: Incentives and purposes. *Educational Policy, 17*(4), 478–502.

Lyne, H. (2005). The Mission Hill School. In T. Hatch, D. Ahmed, A. Lieberman, D. Faigenbaum, M. Eiler White, & D. Pointer Mace (Eds.), *Going public with our teaching: An anthology of practice* (pp. 70–76). New York: Teachers College Press.

Lyne, H. (2010a). *The Mission Hill School.* Retrieved from http://gallery.carnegief-oundation.org/collections/castl_k12/hlyne/

Lyne, H. (2010b). *Redemption.* Retrieved from http://gallery.carnegiefoundation.org/collections/castl_k12/hlyne/redemption.pdf

Mann, H. (1989). *On the art of teaching.* Carlisle, MA: Applewood Books.

Massachusetts Department of Elementary and Secondary Education. (2012). *School and district profiles: MA Department of Elementary and Secondary Education.* http://profiles.doe.mass.edu/profiles/student.aspx?orgcode=00350382&orgtypeco%20de=6&&fycode=2012

McLaren, P. (2006). *Life in schools: An introduction to critical pedagogy in the foundations of education* (5th ed.). Boston: Allyn & Bacon.

McLaughlin, G. B. (2005). Reflections on a descriptive review. *Schools: Studies on Education, 2*(2). 173–182.

McLaughlin, G. B. (2009, Spring). *Six, going on sixteen.* Milwaukee, WI: Rethinking Schools.

McLaughlin, G. B. (2012). *Empowered by play.* Retrieved from http://www.empoweredbyplay.org/

McNeil, L. (1986). *Contradictions of control.* New York: Routledge & Kegan Paul.

McNeil, L. (2000). *Contradictions of school reform: Educational costs of standardization.* New York: Routledge.

Meier, D. (1995). *The power of their ideas: Lessons for America from a small school in Harlem.* Boston: Beacon Press.

Meier, D. (2000). *Can standards save public education?* Boston: Beacon Press.

Meier, D. (2002). *In schools we trust: Creating communities of learning in an era of testing and standardization.* Boston: Beacon Press.

Meier, D. (2012). *Published writings by Deborah Meier.* Retrieved from http://www.deborahmeier.com/Biblio.htm

Meier, D., & Ravitch, D. (2012). *Bridging differences.* Retrieved from http://blogs.edweek.org/edweek/Bridging-Differences/

Meier, D., Sizer, T., & Sizer, N. F. (2004). *Keeping school: Letters to families from principals of two small schools.* Boston: Beacon Press.

Meier, D., Engel, B. S., & Taylor, B. (2010). *Playing for keeps: Life and learning on a public school playground.* New York: Teachers College Press.

Meier, D., & Wood, G. (Eds.). (2004). *Many children left behind: How the No Child Left Behind Act is damaging our children and our schools.* Boston: Beacon Press.

Mills, C. (1999). *The racial contract.* Ithaca, NY: Cornell University Press.

Mission Hill School. (2012). *Our mission.* Retrieved from http://www.missionhillschool.org/mhs/Mission.html

Molnar, A. (2001). *Giving kids the business: The commercialization of America's schools.* Boulder, CO: Westview Press.

Molnar, A. (2005). *School commercialism: From democratic ideal to market commodity.* New York: Routledge.

National Board for Professional Teaching Standards (NBPTS). (2010). *Generalist/middle childhood standards.* Retrieved from http://www.nbpts.org/the_standards/standards_by_cert?ID=27&x=46&y=5

National Commission on Teaching and America's Future. (2007). *The high cost of teacher turnover.* New York: National Commission on Teaching and America's Future.

Noguera, P. A. (2003). *City schools and the American dream: Reclaiming the promise of public education.* New York: Teachers College Press.

Noguera, P. A. (2009). *The trouble with black boys: And other reflections on race, equity, and the future of public education.* San Francisco: Jossey-Bass.

Orfield, G. (2009). *Reviving the goal of an integrated society: A 21st century challenge.* Los Angeles, CA: The Civil Rights Project. Retrieved from http://www.projectcensored.org/top-stories/articles/2-us-schools-are-more-segregated-today-than-in-the-1950s-source/

Orfield, G., & Eaton, S. (1996). *Dismantling desegregation.* New York: New Press.

Orfield, G., Losen, D., Wald, J., & Swanson, C. (2004). *Losing our future.* Cambridge: Harvard Civil Rights Project.

Paley, V. G. (1993). *You can't say you can't play.* Cambridge, MA: Harvard University Press.

Pedroni, T. (2007). *Market movements: African American involvement in school voucher reform.* New York: Routledge.

Perry, T., Steele, C., & Hilliard, A. (2003). *Young, gifted, and black: Promoting high achievement among African-American students.* Boston: Beacon Press.

Peters, D. (2000). *Taking cues from kids: How they think, what to do about it.* Portsmouth, NH: Heinemann.

Piaget, J. (1941). *The child's conception of number.* London: Routledge & Kegan Paul.

Piaget, J. (1973). *To understand is to invent: The future of education.* New York: Grossman.

Piaget, J., & Inhelder, B. (2000). The psychology of the child (2nd ed.). New York: Basic Books.

Pinker, S. (1997). *How the mind works.* New York: Norton.

Raywid, M. A. (1997). Small schools: A reform that works. *Educational Leadership, 55*(4), 35–39.

Raywid, M. A. (1999). *Current literature on small schools.* ERIC ED425029.

Raywid, M. A. (2006). Theme that serves schools well: Small high schools organized around themes are distinguished by engaged students and collaborative faculties. *Phi Delta Kappan, 87*(9), 654–656.

Rothstein, R. (2004). *Class and schools: Using social, economic, and educational reform to close the black-white achievement gap.* New York: Economic Policy Institute, Teachers College, Columbia University.

Sacks, P. (1999). *Standardized minds: The high price of America's testing culture and what we can do to change it.* New York: Perseus Publishing.

Schmoker, M. J., & Wilson, R. B. (1993). *Total quality education: Profiles of schools that demonstrate the power of Deming's management principles.* Bloomington, IN: Phi Delta Kappa Educational Foundation.

Schneider, M., Teske, P. & Marschall, M. (2000). *Choosing schools: Consumer choice and the quality of American schools.* Princeton, NJ: Princeton University Press.

Selden, S. (1999). *Inheriting shame: The story of eugenics and racism in America.* New York: Teachers College Press.

Seller, M. S. (1994). *Women educators in the United States, 1820–1993: A bio-bibliographical sourcebook.* New York: Greenwood Press.

Shekerjian, D. (1990). *Uncommon genius: How great ideas are born.* New York: Penguin Books.

Singleton, G., & Linton, C. W. (2005). *Courageous conversations about race: A field guide for achieving equity in schools.* Thousand Oaks, CA: Corwin.

Snow, C., Griffin, P., & Burns, M. S. (2005). *Knowledge to support the teaching of reading.* San Francisco: Jossey-Bass.

Snyder, J., Lieberman, A., Macdonald, M., & Goodwin, A. (1992). *Makers of meaning in a learning-centered school: A case study of Central Park East 1 Elementary School.* New York: National Center for Restructuring Education, Schools, and Teaching.

Straughter, B. (2001). *The effects of peer observation on self-governance among elementary school teachers* (Unpublished doctoral dissertation). Johnson & Wales University, Providence, RI.

Taber, D. (2011, December 9). School move fight continues. *Mission Hill Gazette,* Retrieved from http://missionhillgazette.com/2011/12/09/school-move-fight-continues/

Taylor, J. F. (2006). *The survival guide for kids with ADD or ADHD.* Minneapolis, MN: Free Spirit Publishing.

Taylor, S. J. (1998). *Desegregation in Boston and Buffalo: The influence of local leaders.* Albany: State University of New York Press.

Teo, T. (2005). *The critique of psychology: From Kant to postcolonial theory.* New York: Springer Science+Business Media.

United States Census Bureau. (2008). *People and households.* Retrieved from http://www.census.gov

United States Public Health Service. (2012). *Mental health: A report of the surgeon general.* Retrieved from http://www.surgeongeneral.gov/library/mentalhealth/chapter3/sec4.html

Valdes, G. (1996). *Con respeto: Bridging the distances between culturally diverse families and schools.* New York: Teachers College Press.

Valenzuela, A. (1999). *Subtractive schooling: U.S.-Mexican youth and the politics of caring.* Albany: State University of New York Press.

Vergari, S. (2007). The politics of charter schools. *Educational Policy, 21*(1), 15–39.

Vygotsky, L. (1978). *Mind in society: The development of higher psychological processes.* Cambridge, MA: Harvard University Press.

Vygotsky, L. (1986). *Thought and language.* Cambridge, MA: MIT Press.

Wein, C. A. (Ed.). (2008). *Emergent curriculum in the primary classroom: Interpreting the Reggio Emilia approach in schools.* New York: Teachers College Press.

Weiner, L. (2005). Neoliberalism, teacher unionism, and the future of public education. *New Politics, 10*(2), 1–18.

Wenger, E. (1999). *Communities of practice: Learning, meaning and identity.* New York: Cambridge University Press.

Wenger, E., McDermott, R., & Snyder, W. M. (2002). *Cultivating communities of practice.* Cambridge, MA: Harvard Business Review Press.

Williams, J. (2011). Jenerra Williams. In S. Chaltain (Ed.), *Faces of learning: 50 powerful stories of defining moments in education* (pp. 90–91). San Francisco: Jossey-Bass.

Wood, G. (1992). *Schools that work: America's most innovative public education programs.* New York: Plume.

Zeichner, K. (2009). *Teacher education and the struggle for social justice.* New York: Routledge.

Index

About the Author

Matthew Knoester (pronounced "canoe-stir") is an assistant professor of education at the University of Evansville. A National Board Certified Teacher and former teacher at the Mission Hill School in Boston, among other schools, he received his master's degree in education from Harvard University and a PhD in curriculum and instruction at the University of Wisconsin–Madison. He edited the book *International Struggles for Critical Democratic Education* and has published articles in a variety of journals, including *Educational Policy, Journal of Adolescent and Adult Literacy*, and *Schools: Studies in Education.*